WHEN THE BOUGH BREAKS

Unearthing the Roots of Postpartum Depression

Patrice,
    Thank you for your continued
love and support; and for
always being a friend.
        Be well,
            Laray ♡

LARAY E. DYER

CONTENTS

DEDICATION

This book is dedicated to:

Mothers we have lost to postpartum depression like Stanlee A. Holbrook, my inspiration for this book:

According to the Pittsburgh Post-Gazette, "Pittsburgh police said Stanlee Allyn Holbrook, 26, parked on the bridge around 7:20 p.m. and left three children inside the vehicle before jumping over the railing" (June 17, 2019). But like so many of us, there's more to her story. As told by  her loving sister, Janet Zigler, "Many people would think that my sister was alone. She was never alone--we talked, and she spent every day with my mother and me. She had a family that cared and loved her deeply. Not to mention, Stanlee had a gang of friends." Read more of the untold story of the late Stanlee A. Holbrook in Appendix A.

This book is also dedicated to:

Women who suffer from postpartum depression. Although it may feel like it, you are not alone. There is an army of women who have been where you are and successfully overcame; or are yet believing to see rest on the other side of exhaustion and joy on the other side of sadness. I encourage you to speak up and ask for the support you need. With help, you can get through this!

Sisters who have experienced and overcame postpartum depression, and graciously share their stories with us like Kholiwe Dlamini, Maureen Dyer, LuShaun Falconer, Anana Harris Parris, Chanel Martin and De'Anna Reaves. You not only make a difference in my journey, but also inspire countless women to never lose hope. There is transformative power in your story. Thank you for offering it within this text. Read their stories in Appendix B.

Family and friends that love us regardless like Lynn Scott (my mother) and Silbert (Dave) Dyer (my husband). Without hesitation, Dave and my mom partnered together to support me in the birth of both Melody and Malakai. Following each delivery, I was readmitted to the hospital, entrusting my mom to care for my brand-new babies, which allowed my husband to be by my side. I am forever grateful to my mom and Dave, my sisters, Camille and Marianna, and my friends for their love and support.

Providers or more appropriately, my phenomenal, integrated care team consisting of Drs. Kurt Martinuzzi and Heather Silver (Emory Clinic); Drs. Toby Goldsmith and Lauren Schmidt (Emory Women's Mental Health Program); Dr. Glen Egan (Emory Brain Health Center), Drs. Timothy Moore and Tamara Almeyda, as well as, the entire team at the Adult Intensive Outpatient Program (Emory University Hospital at Wesley Woods); Jenny Barwick, LPC, CPCS (Searching for Vitality Counseling); Motherwise Support Group (Atlanta Birthing Center); and Alicia C. Simpson MS, RD, IBCLC, LD and Catherine Palmer, IBCLC (Pea Pod Nutrition and Lactation Support).

Despite two successful births, for a long time, I suffered in silence—before, during, and after the delivery of my children. I lost a little one and suffered even more. But with your support and attention, I no longer suffer alone and am healing. Sincere thanks to all of you for your care. In turn, dear ones, "I hope all is well with you and that you are as healthy in body as you are strong in spirit" (3 John 1:2)

ACKNOWLEDGEMENTS

In completing my inaugural work, I owe a debt of gratitude to those who helped make it happen. Foremost, I want to acknowledge Nia Akinyemi. Nia helped me gather my thoughts and hone them into an outline; she also coached me along the way and guided me through the self-publishing process. Thank you, Nia!

I am also indebted to Chanel Martin for empowering me to "just write." I began the process of writing during her seven-day writing challenge; and completed my book during her twenty-one-day bootcamp; Chanel also equipped me with a sales, marketing, and public relations strategy. Thanks, Chanel!

Finally, I want to appreciate my husband, Dave. For a season, most nights, I retreated to my office to write, leaving him alone or to look after and care for our children. Dave's support and encouragement is undying and indeed, a labor of love. Thanks a lot, babe. I love you too.

FOREWORD

I have been a therapist for over a decade now. Before starting my own practice, I worked in the hospital setting serving adults and geriatric patients with severe or moderate mood disorders. I left the hospital to start my own practice.

While I still love working with geriatric patients and general mood disorders, over the years, I developed an interest in a population called "maternal mental health". It covers everything from infertility, pregnancy loss, and postpartum mood disorders to infant loss and everything in between. However, something that intrigued me was that postpartum mood disorders occur in 1 out of every 7 women. That seemed outrageous to me!

Postpartum depression is more than what you see in the media—it is a very serious type of depression, but also a very treatable type of depression. It is important for anyone reading this to know that postpartum depression does NOT equal women hating their children. It also should be dealt with by a provider with specific training as this population is very different from generalized depression.

That being said ...I have seen a lot of people in my career. I met Laray April 2019. She was by far one of the MOST depressed clients I have ever seen in my career. Here is this beautiful lady, with a gorgeous new baby boy, and she can hardly make it to my office. She looked like she had not showered in several days, deep bags under both eyes.

My office is in a building built before ADA was a thing, and there are several stairs, no elevator. She sat down and told me she hoped I was on the ground level, but then realized I was on the top. Once in the suite, she saw more stairs and said she hoped I was on the main level in the suite—again, disappointed because I'm on the top of the suite as well. When she finally sat down and got settled, she began to tell her story. She looked at me and asked, "am I a good enough mother?" and began to cry. That question comes up often in this population. And my response is always, "absolutely."

As we began to work together, I found Laray to be such an incredible client. All she wanted was to feel better, understand what she was feeling, and get back to her life. In postpartum mood depression, there is usually a deep level of shame that exudes from the person. Laray didn't want to hurt her son, she enjoyed being around him, but she did struggle with transitioning to be a mother of two, wife, and eventually going back to work.

Therapy is not an easy journey, but it's one that takes honesty, patience, perseverance, and hope. I invite anyone reading this, to remember you are not alone, your story matters, you matter.

Jenny Barwick, LPC, CPCS

Searching for Vitality, LLC

678.343.5308

jsbarwicklpc@gmail.com

INTRODUCTION

Do You Know That You're Depressed?

"Focus solely on the physical well-being of the pregnant woman is not adequate for healthy mother-child outcomes. Prenatal intervention requires a more holistic view, taking into consideration not only the physical realm, but the psychological and emotional realms, as well."[1]

Document Date: March 26, 2019 13:33

Document Title: Postpartum Check

Performed By: Martinuzzi, Kurt W.

History of Present Illness

Laray is a 41-year-old married, African American female. She has been pregnant 3 times. Patient is tearful. She has a history of depression and was on Zoloft, but she stopped this during the pregnancy. She also stopped her talk therapy. Edinburgh Score: 15 (Patient called the office to set up an appointment with psychiatry),

Assessment/Plan

Postpartum Depression; will start Zoloft this evening. The patient will gradually increase her dose to 100 mg daily at bedtime. The patient called the office to set up talk therapy. We will have her out of work until her depression is dissolved.

I am a first-generation college graduate with a Bachelor of Arts degree in Political Science from Hampton University (2000), a Master of Science degree in Public Policy and Management from Carnegie Mellon University (2002) and a Master of Divinity degree with a joint concentration in Faith & Health and Black Church Studies from Emory University (2010). I am a certified Project Management Professional with the Project Management Institute and a certified Health Coach with the Institute for Integrative Nutrition. Most importantly, I am an Ordained Minister, wife, and mother of two.

For all intents and purposes, I appear to have it all together, at least on the outside. But when you begin to peer beyond how I look—smart, put together, how I sound—calm and educated, and my movement—casual and relaxed, a duality of sorts comes to light. Despite my background, what seems to be truer to my day-to-day experience is that I am a Black woman who suffered a severe case of postpartum depression and is still recovering. According to the Centers for Disease Control and Prevention, "postpartum depression estimates...can be as high as 1 in 5 women." Moreover, PPD disproportionately affects African American women than other groups.

Recently, following the birth of my amazing son, Malakai (2019), a happy baby that shows off his two teeth and gums at every opportunity, I experienced Postpartum Depression (PPD). PPD, one of the most common medical complications during and after pregnancy, typically arises from a combination of hormonal changes, psychological adjustment to motherhood and fatigue.

The signs and symptoms of PPD can be physical, emotional and/or behavioral. For me, it was all the above. I remember walking into the doctor's office for my six-week check-up like it was yesterday. Baby in tow, I was a nervous wreck. My anxiety was at an all-time high; I wasn't eating nor sleeping. In fact, I was so exhausted that I wanted to kill myself. I had so much on my mind but could hardly think straight. I felt very sad and even more overwhelmed. I was worried about returning to work—train wreck that I was—because I didn't think I'd be able to maintain my workload. It's no wonder that I was irritable beyond measure, not wanting to be bothered with anyone or anything, including my sweet baby. I just wasn't myself and didn't feel confident that I could return to business as usual.

When Dr. Kurt Martinuzzi walked into the room, tears began to fall. I had a history with him. After seven days of severe preeclampsia following the birth of my gifted daughter, Melody (2015), a sassy toddler with enough personality to carry a room, Dr. Martinuzzi made the call that finally tamped down my blood pressure (I'm convinced he saved my life). He also shepherded me through the loss of a little one and advised my husband and I on conceiving again; and finally, he was my primary obstetrician throughout my pregnancy with Malakai. Dr. Martinuzzi warmly greeted me and helped me unpack my concerns. He gave me a questionnaire to take and then left the room. When he returned, he said, "Your score is terrible! Do you know that you're depressed?" Rather than coming to terms with this reality, I explained to Dr. Martinuzzi that it was time for me to return to work (in other words, I didn't have time to be depressed) and he confirmed what I already knew—I was in no condition to work.

Dr. Martinuzzi equipped me with every resource that I would need to overcome PPD. He instructed me to resume antidepressants and seek the guidance of psychiatry to adjust my medication, as needed. He gave me the number for psychotherapy and stood by as I called to schedule a consultation for talk therapy. Finally, he called my husband and explained the seriousness of my condition—a condition that ultimately led to outpatient psychiatric care with Transitions Behavioral Health Programs, a part of Emory University Hospital at Wesley Woods.

The mission of Transitions is "to deliver superior mental health services to adults in the hospital setting and to promote the concepts of dignity and empowerment while serving the mental health needs of patients." I participated in the Adult Intensive Outpatient Program (IOP) where I was supported by a multidisciplinary clinical team to address the emotional and mental distress I was experiencing. Like the bout of PPD that I faced following the birth of Melody, I was overcome, debilitated in a way that made the simplest task, like brushing my teeth, feel like climbing Mount Everest. But this time, I was seeking help. Unaddressed PPD can have harmful, long-term effects on mothers, their babies, and their family members. In the US, about 50% of PPD cases may go undiagnosed.

With the support of my loving husband, Dave, my family and friends, and the aid of medication, psychotherapy, intensive outpatient therapy, a psychological evaluation, support groups, critical self-care and spiritual practice, I overcame. It is this more intimate, delicate story that I care to share: my journey through a mental health crisis and beyond.

I believe there are many risk factors that made me susceptible to PPD—a history of depression, a prior episode of postpartum depression, psychological stress, complications following childbirth, and perceiving a lack of support. For the purpose of this memoir, I will focus on my history with depression, sharing my initial onset and life experiences that led me to PPD. I will also share how my spiritual beliefs initially impacted my perception of interventions and how maternity exacerbated the depression, leading to a mental health crisis. Finally, I will elaborate on my treatment plan and road to recovery, including how I participated in and advocated for my mental health and well-being.

Provided is a summary of each section of this book:

- Section one focuses on my early years and identifies the historical factors that contributed to early incidence of and predisposition to depression.
- Section two captures the formation of my identity and provides insight into my faith journey.
- Section three accounts for the more recent mental health factors that led me to crisis, diagnosis and healing.
- Section four focuses on my continuous pursuit toward mental/emotional health, including basic self-care, enhanced self-care and next steps.

In revealing my story, my goal is to provide experiential insight into best practices and interventions for cultivating and sustaining mental health and well-being, especially during a crisis.

SIGNS OF POSTPARTUM DEPRESSION

Physical

- Physical aches and pains
- Changes in appetite
- Lack of sleep or oversleeping
- Difficulty concentrating

Emotional

- Feeling sad, hopeless, empty, or overwhelmed
- Crying more often than usual or for no apparent reason
- Feeling worried or overly anxious
- Moodiness, restlessness, or irritability
- Anger or rage
- Persistent doubt about your ability to care for your baby
- Thoughts of harming yourself or your baby

Behavioral

- Loss of interest in things that are usually enjoyable
- Avoiding friends and family
- Having trouble bonding or forming an emotional attachment with your baby

PART ONE

Herstory: Remembering the Past

"The itsy-bitsy spider
Climbed up the waterspout
Down came the rain
And washed the spider out."[2]
"Our relationships, especially with our parents, are reevaluated with each new baby."[3]

Born to Lynn and Larry Scott in 1978, a thirty something couple who, though never married, held themselves in the community as husband and wife, my upbringing seemed as "normal" as any other five-year-old black girl growing up in the urban, East Liberty neighborhood of Pittsburgh, Pennsylvania. My mother, a gorgeous, slender, calm spirit, often donning caftans or terry cloth jumpsuit, was a stellar stay-at-home mom. She took care of my older sister, Camille, and I in a way that I can only aspire to take care of my Melody and Malakai. When Camille and I left out for school, we were well put together—hair freshly styled, bodies clean and moisturized, clothes neat and ironed; and when we arrived home, the house was warm and inviting—smelling of something homemade. My mom loved us dearly and imparted everything she was into making us the women we are today. She remains a gem.

Camille and I went to Lemington Elementary. Lemington felt so big yet I felt safe at school because Camille, both confident and athletic, was the crossing guard. She sported an iridescent orange sash like she was Miss America and could stop traffic on a dime. Camille seemed invincible, and I knew she would not only protect me in traffic but also in life. Everything she was I wanted to be—outgoing, charismatic and fearless. Her leadership transcended family—it created, for me, a sense of community.

Within this community, just down the hill from our 1920's home, was a big red firehouse. Knowing that firemen were a skip, hop, and jump away made me feel secure, as did the neighborhood kids who looked out for me—at least until the street lights came on. But no one made me feel more secure than my daddy.

My dad, quiet in nature, talked in a low tone and had a great sense of humor. Though working-class—a mechanic by trade, he provided for us well. My memories with my daddy are few but precious:

...I remember going past his garage after school and almost always finding him up under a car. It was cool and intriguing to me. I would stoop down low to greet him and he would roll out from under the car on what looked like a skateboard to return the exchange. Later, he would come home covered in and stinking of grease. He'd shower in the basement and then come up and join us for dinner. When I finished my dinner, I would retreat under the table and sit at his feet.

...I remember Christmas—how my dad must have picked the first tree he saw. It was short and round. It had to be cheap, but it smelled like Christmas and as we dressed it in blue lights and silver tinsel, the joy of Christmas filled the house. We were all excited on Christmas morning. Mom, Camille and I beat dad downstairs, so he came running down the steps—slipped, fell, and slid to the bottom. Once we realized that he was ok, we laughed until we cried. He swears the carpet moved but I'm still not convinced.

...I remember Saturday mornings with my dad. He would make sugar toast—white bread with butter and granulated sugar set under the broiler. The sugar was caramelized, sweet and crispy on the top and the bread remained soft and fluffy on the bottom (I still make it when I'm feeling nostalgic). He'd then watch cartoons with me and rock me in an oversized brown leather rocking chair with a heavy steel frame. I'd try to rock in it alone when he wasn't around, but it didn't rock the same; there was nothing like rocking with my daddy. Nothing.

...I remember living with my dad... and then I didn't.

Up until the summer of 1983, my mom and dad provided a solid familial and communal environment for Camille and me to thrive; we had each other, and that was everything. But one exceptional day, that changed—my mother packed our belongings and left my dad. I imagine I helped pack and didn't think much of it. Then, my cousin Brian came over with a truck and began to load our boxes. Again, nothing seemed too much out of the ordinary to me until Brian picked up my daddy's oversized brown leather rocking chair with a heavy steel frame. My mother stopped him and said, "That stays here." In that moment, I realized that we were moving but my daddy was not coming with us. My five-year-old self was broken to the core—not only was I losing my friends and a sense of community but also my daddy. This was my first and most significant breakdown—colored with deep grief and emotional trauma—and the lens through which most of my life was subsequently lived. Father absence harms children.

Despite the absenteeism of my dad and the daddy-sized void that only seemed to grow as I aged, I had a healthy childhood. My mom, Camille, and I moved into a brand-new townhouse on the North Side and I quickly made new friends. Sharron Russell, a devout Jehovah's Witness, was my new best friend. We did everything together from riding bikes, to going to see the candy lady and jumping double dutch until dusk. Although I was Baptist, my mom would even let me attend her family's home-based bible study and visit Kingdom Hall with Sharron.

My mom transitioned from at-home to working full-time for the major league baseball team, the Pittsburgh Pirates. I fondly think of and remember the thrill of baseball games and the players who made time for Camille and me both on and off the field—Bobby Bonilla, RJ Reynolds, Barry Bonds, Bill Madlock, Tony Penya, and Johnny Rae, to name a few. During one game, Bobby was injured so he and his family sat with us and we watched the game together. Out of nowhere, a foul ball was headed straight toward me, but Bobby stretched across two people and caught it before it could make contact. This is just one of many examples where the players came through for Camille and me. In sharing time with them, I see my five-year-old self trying to remember what it feels like to be a whole family and to live in community; even at six- and seven-years old, the ache of missing daddy was paramount.

"When I think of home
I think of a place where there's love overflowing.
I wish I was home
I wish I was back there with the things I been knowing."[4]

My mother was smart and driven—she never seemed to miss a beat. Though she struggled as a single-parent, it wouldn't be apparent to Camille and me until later in life. For two years, my mother did all that she could to mitigate the breakdown of our family and support us. Initially, I think my dad tried to help her and maintain his relationship with Camille and I, but for reasons unknown, making and keeping his promise quickly became more than he could manage. Shortly thereafter my father moved to California. I felt like he no longer wanted to be in relationship with me and didn't value our father-daughter bond. According to the National Fatherhood Initiative, there is a crisis in America of fatherless children. That is, "19.7 million children, more than 1 in 4, live without a father in the home."[5] Consequently, we see a plethora of societal ills that affect children raised in father-absent homes: poverty, teen pregnancy, behavioral problems, obesity, and crime, to name a few. Though superficially happy, I withdrew from my friends and began to favor protective male relationships. I no longer felt secure in my identity. A father is supposed to instill in his daughter who she is, but my father was no longer available to impart in me, which made me increasingly vulnerable as I aged. Low self-esteem and insecurity were my portion as I experienced the physical, emotional, and behavioral effects of being a fatherless daughter, especially depression. Indeed, I was devastated and more so disturbed by the abrupt end of my close relationship with my father. I know for sure that this breakdown changed the trajectory of my life and my predisposition for depression and anxiety, as would the next transition.

"In 1909, Milton and Catherine Hershey established a residential school to provide a positive, structured home life year-round to help children gain the skills to be successful in all aspects of life."[6]

Again, my mother did all that she could to mitigate the effects of the separation and support me and Camille; ultimately, she sent us to Milton Hershey School (MHS), a boarding school in Hershey, PA. This change demolished the structure once known as my family—my heart now ached for my dad, my mom, and my sister (she and I were placed in different homes). At the same time, it reconstructed my involvement within a nuclear family. Consequently, for me, MHS, situated on 3,340 acres of farmland, was a breath of fresh air—like going to summer camp only better. I knew my mom would remain actively in my life and bring my sister and I together as much as she could.

When I arrived at my student home, Grant, I was greeted by a friendly white couple, Mr. and Mrs. Mortonson, who advised that I could call them mom and pop. I was then introduced to 12 other girls and boys from all over the world. We engaged in the home like brothers and sisters. I loved the Mortonson's and my new family. Mom Mortonson was nothing short of a modern-day June Clever meets Mary Poppins. I fondly remember she and the children greeting me with, "Consider Yourself" from the 1960 original Broadway musical Oliver!

"Consider yourself at home

Consider yourself one of the family

We've taken to you so strong

It's clear we're going to get along

Consider yourself well in

Consider yourself part of the furniture

There isn't a lot to spare

Who cares? Whatever we've got, we share!"

The sound of music could always be heard. Sadly, during my stint at Grant, the Mortonson's retired. Again, my family was fractured, and I was devastated but the Bushby's replaced the Mortonson's and were equally as lovely.

Attending MHS brought the notion of nuclear family back into balance for me. I received a good education, a sense of stability and security, and flourished accordingly. The greatest gift MHS gave me, aside from encouragement to continue to explore my belief in God through Sunday worship (I can still hear the organ with gigantic pipes playing beautiful, melodious hymns), bible reading and prayer, was an appreciation for diversity. I lived, played, and went to school with a very diverse population—children from all over the world. For example, my best friend Mai Mai was Asian. She once received a care package from her folks, and I remember sitting on the porch with her trying seaweed for the first time. It was thin, crisp and salty—and seemed to melt on my tongue.

I saw Camille once a week in passing after Sunday worship. Too cool for school, she would typically shoo me away as she would congregate with her friends; she was still my hero. As we aged, I think I became more of a nuisance to her, but she never stopped looking out for me. We attended MHS for five years—I transitioning from junior to intermediate division and she from intermediate to senior. Once again, I was on the move from Mom and Pop Bushby and the boys and girls I had grown to love at Grant to Mr. and Mrs. Graham and twelve other girls at Oak Grove. Shifting from calling my house parent's Mom and Pop to calling them Mr. and Mrs. caused the warmth of family to wax cold; Mrs. Graham was stern, and I was of age to accept that she was not my mother.

A good friend of Camille's, Dikesha, was living at Oak Grove when I arrived, and she looked out for me as Camille would. Dikesha, kind, sweet and responsible, was Mrs. Graham's favorite—she could do no wrong. I, on the other hand, began to act out, consistently receiving detentions and restrictions. I was almost always restricted from cookies at bedtime, but Dikesha oversaw distributing the cookies and always smuggled couple for me. But soon, Dikesha moved on to senior division and I was moved from home to home.

My mother and grandmother, a strong, proud woman who also had a deliberate hand in raising me, was a classy, sophisticated woman with a heart for people. She would visit Camille and I about once a month. They would take us off campus to the mall and out to eat. My connections with my mother and grandmother never wavered, and certainly never broke. I strongly believe my grandmother, made it her personal mission to fill my daddy-sized void and she showed up heroically in every area of my life. Sadly, only my father could fill that space, and though he called me from time to time, nothing was the same.

In the spring of 1991 while home on spring break, I became seriously ill. My mother took me to Children's Hospital in Oakland twice, but they kept sending me home. By the end of the week, my medium-brown skin had turned dark brown with a green undertone and became rough like a lizard. Not knowing what else to do, my mom and grandfather, a gentle giant in heart, drove me four hours to the clinic at MHS. Upon examination, they immediately rushed me to Hershey Medical Center where I had emergency surgery. It turns out that my appendix had ruptured earlier in the week and the toxins were poisoning my system. I could have died. I was hospitalized for three months. Then came the end of the academic year. Camille was set to graduate from MHS and head to college; so, my mother gave me the option to stay at MHS or return home with her. I chose to go home.

"Maybe there's a chance for me to go back there
Now that I have some direction
It would sure be nice to be back home
Where there's love and affection
And just maybe I can convince time to slow up
Giving me enough time in my life to grow up
Time be my friend, let me start again." [7]

When I arrived home, I gave my life to Christ. I had received a card from my home church, Mt. Ararat Baptist Church, when I was hospitalized. I knew I had folks praying for me and ventured to think it was those prayers that brought me through. I remember Rev. Donald O. Clay, Jr. extending an altar call. As I rose and headed down the center aisle toward the front, our eyes met and he announced to the congregation, "This is a miracle child here!" Because my grandmother was highly regarded and well known as a pillar in the church and community, so too was my story.

Familial and communal belonging are essential components to mental health and well-being, especially among youth. Too many disruptions or breakdowns therein can and will eventually lead to distress in the mind, body and spirit, if not addressed appropriately. Almost like the prodigal son, I returned home to my family and was baptized into a community of believers with the hope of healing and wholeness. Once again, back with family, back in community. Little did I know that I would need the Holy Spirit for what I was about to encounter.

"Each day we stood almost shoulder to shoulder, occupying the same space, breathing the same air, but we remained strangers."[8]

"For I was hungry, and you gave Me no food; I was thirsty, and you gave Me no drink; I was a stranger, and you did not take Me in." (Matthew 25:42-43, KJV)

Once I settled in at home, I found that home was different. My daddy was gone, and I was experiencing what relationship expert Iyanla Vanzant calls the 7 "Uns" of Daddyless Daughters: feeling unwanted, unloved, unlovable, unacceptable, unimportant, unattractive, and unworthy.[9] Camille had gone off to Tuskegee University, my mother now worked to provide for she and I, and I felt somewhat on an island.

My mom rented a nice, two-bedroom apartment in the North Hills suburbs of Pittsburgh. Consequently, I attended predominantly white middle and high schools. To be clear, when I say predominantly white, I mean of the "1,036 students at the high school, 10 are Black. In the entire district, 64 of 4,644 students are Black."[10] Having been raised on a farm by white couples, and living with white children as sisters and brothers, this was of no significance to me. However, the feeling was not mutual. I quickly learned this when I found the cryptic letters KKK etched in my locker and my pink notebook. On another occasion, "f--k niggers, go home" was spray painted on the stairwell wall. The janitor tried to clean it off, but the blue spray paint stained the grout and served as a constant reminder of this act of hatred.

One day, upon getting caught up with friends in the lunch line, I neglected to move up. I then heard from behind me, "Move up nigger!" I was so taken aback that I immediately spun around and boldly said "Who called me a nigger?" I wanted someone to take responsibility! I learned that it was Butch, a racist bully. I also learned that he would not take responsibility alone; adding insult to injury, I too was suspended for 5-days for using the n-word. Knowing my history, my mother felt every bit of my pain. Initially, she'd come up to my school to comfort and console me, but this day it was clear she'd had enough. In my presence, my mother told my principal, Mr. McCurry, "If my daughter can't go here, no one will; I'll burn it down!" I'd never seen my mom so radical. I felt empowered—at least that day—but mostly, I felt scared. I served my suspension.

These events were well covered locally, nationally and internationally on BET News channels and its affiliates, as well as, in print:

"They detailed numerous racist incidents in which black students were called racial slurs, spat at, and taunted by a group of white students. 'I am afraid. I feel unsafe in the building,' 10th-grader Laray Scott said. Scott's friend, Malika Redmond, also a sophomore, echoed those sentiments. 'We are requesting more security at the school,' said Redmond, who was hoping the board would hire additional security staff for the building" (April 6, 1994).[11] These events were not isolated rather, indicative of the acceptable culture of racial and ethnic intimidation at North Hills. I endured it for four years, but I didn't do so quietly. My friend Malika and I founded the diversity council to educate students on different cultures. We, along with our mothers, also led the school board in drafting a racial, ethnic, and religious intimidation policy to underscore our efforts. Nevertheless, I remained a target of hate. John, the school security guard, escorted me to and from class. Having grown from the naive girl that believed family and community are made in the heart, I now know what it meant to be a stranger. My grief accumulated.

"I don't like to go to school anymore," added Scott, who said she had missed 2½ days of school this month because of other incidents and feared for her safety. "I know I have to keep up because I'm already behind. It just drains me. This is just so stressful, she said in an interview yesterday." Her mother, Lynn Scott, said a group of Black parents planned to meet with [Superintendent] Esais once a month. 'This is an issue we must address. It has gone on for too long, and people must be educated,' Lynn Scott said, her voice rising" (March 25, 1994). [12]

"Racism is a social determinant of health that has a profound impact on the health status of children, adolescents, emerging adults, and their families."[13] It fosters sickness and dis-ease. So, who and where was my community? Was there a balm for the trauma I endured? My instinct said my Gilead was Hampton

University (HU). Was it right?

> *Suddenly my world has changed its face*
> *But I still know where I'm going.*
> *I have had my mind spun around in space*
> *And yet I've watched it growing.*[14]

"We are such idiots; we think everyone else has it all figured out. But we're all stumbling around in dark rooms bumping into furniture and stifling our cries so no one will know."[15]

"Human relations are built on feeling, not on reason or knowledge. And feeling is not an exact science; like all spiritual qualities, it has the vagueness of greatness about it."[16]

I partly remember the day I arrived on the campus of HU. I remember my mom being there and I know my grandma was there too—not because I can place her but because she was always there, present at every important juncture of my life. I remember standing in long lines for admissions, financial aid, registration and for school supplies at Walmart. I also remember owing the university thousands of dollars and racking up quite a tab at Walmart to make my new digs feel like home. I'm sure my grandma effortlessly wrote the check and paid the tab— she'd been working since the age of thirteen and done very well for herself financially and otherwise. When I was born, my grandparents had already divorced, so my only knowledge of my grandmother was as a strong, independent women. She was the matriarch and leader of the family. I aspired to, one day, stand in her shoes.

My roommate, Vanessa, was a quiet, naive, country girl with a strong southern drawl. I somewhat befriended her but found more commonalities with some of the other girls on my floor, especially Nikole. Nikole, too, was from the south but she had an attractive swag and confidence about her, like she'd done this before (although she clearly hadn't). I also befriended Tiffany, a northern girl like me; sweet, pretty and fun to be around. For the first semester of college, we were like the three musketeers. One day, not sure at the time what possessed me, I decided to run for Miss Freshman with my introverted self. So, the three of us posted up outside of the cafeteria, day after day during the campaign, while I smiled and waved, asking random people to vote for me. I ran opposed to an "it" girl named Jocelyn who, rather than carelessly hanging out, strategically enrolled her entire dormitory to vote for her. She won by a landslide and I felt small. Though my college experience was peppered with flighty episodes, more so, it was seasoned with long stints of depression.

One day, Tiffany, Nikole and I decided to visit the boy's dormitories. Somewhere on the journey from our side of campus to theirs, along that beautiful stretch of campus that paralleled the sea, Vanessa spotted us. Thinking she may cramp our style, we ran and eventually lost her—it was a "mean girls" thing to do. In response, Vanessa told my friends, "Everybody thinks Laray has it all together, but she doesn't have it all together." How did she know? Was it the piles of clean laundry scattered around my side of the room or was it the many times Vanessa left for class and returned only to find me still asleep? Her words, though simple, haunted me and still do to this day—not because she spoke them out of spite but because they were and continue to be true. I didn't have it all together then, and I don't have it all together now.

Due to financial issues, Tiffany did not return after the fall semester. I became roommates with Nikole but eventually, we fell out and wouldn't speak for a year. I felt so alone; I was alone. Kirk Cameron said, "Every candle that gets lit in the dark room must feel a little rejection from the darkness around it, but the last thing I want from those who hold a different world view to me is to accept me." I'm not surprised that my predominantly white peers didn't accept me in high school, but I never imagined feeling so isolated at a historically black university. The loneliness was only exacerbated by the pervasive classism at Hampton. I was keenly aware that I had and came from less than my peers and for that, I felt inferior; there are many negative effects of classism.

Again, I slept most days away, and despite being an "A" student, I only went to class enough to carry a "B" average. I didn't socialize much; rather, I kept to myself—ordering my lunch and dinner to go on most days and eating in my room. I can still smell the scent of saran wrap on my turkey sandwich with provolone, spicy mustard, lettuce and tomato; I ate one almost every day for lunch and sometimes for dinner.

For reasons I can't recall, I had a personality conflict with my Public Speaking teacher. I called my mom crying and told her that I wanted to come home. In typical fashion, she supported me and said, then come home but I wasn't ready to give up completely.

"If you're list'ning God

Please don't make it hard to know

If we should believe in the things that we see

Tell us, should we run away

Should we try and stay

Or would it be better just to let things be?"[17]

I did not return to public speaking—I took an "F." I never found my niche at HU; I never found my tribe. Thankfully, however, Nikole and I mended our rift and she proved to be a genuine, lifelong friend. Lakrisha, a kind, sharp, fashionista, also served as a lifesaver, a light in the darkness of my experience. She too remains a good friend. When I graduated from HU, I was relieved to return home and didn't look back.

"Depression and posttraumatic stress disorder (PTSD) share some symptoms. With either one, you might have trouble sleeping, get angry over little things, or lose interest in people or things. Sometimes, you can have both conditions."[18]

For me, enrolling in Carnegie Mellon University was a big break. It was diverse and felt more like MHS than any environment that I'd been in in a long time. It permitted me to live with my grandma and commute back and forth to school. Once again, I had my family to ground me. I also made some friends and did as well as could be expected for a young black woman who barely knew how to check her email now attending the #1 school for information and technology management.[19] I knew that I was in a blessed place that would open many doors for me, and I was grateful.

I was in a good place until the September 11th terrorist attacks. The grand exposure of this horrific tragedy gripped me in the worst way. I had reached my last year at the university and moved into a studio apartment in Shadyside. I can still see myself curled up on my pale-yellow loveseat, covered in a soft throw, watching television and wailing. Mind you, I didn't know anyone in Manhattan, Arlington County, nor Stonycreek Township—I had no personal connection—but I was nonetheless devastated, my heart broken for those injured and killed, and their loved ones.

Though I recognize the possibility that I was experiencing depression and/or PTSD, also at work in me was a palpable formation of God developing my heart for His people. I didn't know what to do with it at the time, how to channel profound grief through prayer. So, like many affixed to all the television coverage, I incessantly watched and wept. The attacks killed 2,996 people, injured over 25,000 others. For countless individuals and the country at-large, home would never be the same.

"Living here, in this brand-new world

Might be a fantasy

But it taught me to love

So it's real, real to me."[20]

Over the years, my vocational goals have evolved from wanting to become a child advocate attorney to a focus on economic development and urban planning, which was my intention when I enrolled in CMU. However, the trend at CMU seemed to lean more toward management consulting and the profit therein. I was a first-generation college graduate, and frankly, didn't know which way to go so I went with the crowd. Some days I regret deciding my career based on earning potential rather than the needs of my community, but in the words of Maya Angelou, I "wouldn't take nothing for my journey now," and fortunately, with my decision came great opportunity.

As my time at CMU came to an end, I participated in several on-campus interviews. One company, AMS, truly sparked my interest. It was competitive but more relaxed than a McKinsey & Company type of firm. I went through two rounds of interviewing and when I received a letter in the mail I was elated; sadly, the letter was one of rejection. I was blue but as time passed, I picked my head up, just in time to receive a call from AMS. One of the students that they'd extended an offer to rescind their acceptance! I didn't care that I wasn't their first choice; I was their current choice and that made all the difference. Once again, I uprooted from my family and relocated to northern Virginia for work.

As mentioned, with my career choice came great opportunity; most notably, a Top-Secret clearance and the chance to contract as an Intelligence Analyst with the Central Intelligence Agency. I worked alongside and supported some of the best and brightest. I enjoyed my work but found that I was lonely and continued to struggle with depression. For the first time, I began to treat the depression with medication.

PART TWO

Balancing Mental Health and Ministry

"My two lives were intertwined, but I saw the seams and felt the frays where they joined. I knew how to live in duality. I knew how to perform and smile while being sad. I lived with both great highs and great lows, and I learned how to hide it."[21]

"Depression is life grief. It's a sadness that creeps in on you and slowly overwhelms you. Sometimes, I feed it like a repast after a funeral; other times, I sing and shout my way through it. But after the relatives leave, and the food is eaten, and the lights go off, it's still there; and it feels so bad that you try to escape it by any means necessary."[22]

In seeking a remedy for depression, I found a faith community—Bibleway Apostolic Church in Alexandria, Virginia. I needed and desired a closer walk with God and a community to support that walk. I found it at Bibleway, a small storefront church led by Pastor Turner. Pastor Turner was strict and very conservative, yet kind in heart. What she preached about on my first visit tugged on me. When she opened the altar for prayer, I made my way to the front of the church. The altar worker asked me a few questions and consequently, escorted me out of the sanctuary for baptism. This time, I wasn't baptized in a beautiful edifice with stained glass windows and tepid water, reminiscent of my adolescence; rather, I was baptized in a cold, dank boiler room, symbolic of the sadness I felt. I went down in the water in Jesus' name and came up ready to receive the Holy Spirit. Having grown up in a more traditional church, this concept was new to me. I'd never heard anyone speak in tongues, let alone experienced it for myself. But, having studied the scripture, I was confident that I wanted this experience and remained opened to the chorus of charismatic folks that surrounded me with tongue talking, clapping, and shouts of praise and thanksgiving. Soon thereafter, my voice joined the chorus, speaking in a language that I'd never been taught and connecting with a community in a way that I'd never been allied. I found much comfort in my faith.

Shortly after rededicating my life to Christ, I moved to Georgia and joined Bethesda Cathedral of the Apostolic Faith Church, serving both Bishop Reese, Jr. and Bishop Reese, III for over a decade. A lot happened in and for me ministerially; a lot also happened with me psychologically and emotionally. I started out in ministry with the choir and working with the youth and young adults. I loved being in the choir under the direction of Lady Reese; it deepened my spiritual experience exponentially. The more songs that I learned, the more I praised and worshipped God, and the more sincere my prayer life became. Despite the social anxiety that I began to experience, I made a point to attend rehearsals and sing in front of the congregation on Sunday morning because it not only blessed God, but also blessed me.

As my heart for God continued to grow, so too did my participation and calling. I fell in love with works of benevolence, evangelism, and especially hospital visitation. I was called to preach and consequently responded to the call by enrolling in seminary at Emory University's Candler School of Theology. While at Candler, as a part of my contextual education requirement, I performed hospital chaplaincy. This experience was intense. I remember visiting with a woman in fourth stage cancer. It didn't take much for her to open up to me and realize that in being strong for her daughters she neglected to feel the fear, isolation, and frailty that her condition imposed. Our time together allowed her to feel again; I offered a shoulder to lean on and a tissue to catch her tears.

I also had the opportunity to bless a baby and comfort two families in the death of loved ones. My heart went out to the new mother, who gave birth alone and had no visitors. I empathized with the deep sadness I identified within her, but her focus was outward on her new baby, ensuring her little one was dedicated to God so, I obliged. I also had the privilege of supporting two families in discovering the loss of their loved one. Picture a woman working on a home project with her husband who runs off to Home Depot and never returns. It turns out, he dropped dead in the store. She was furious with him, bewailing that they were supposed to grow old together and sit in rocking chairs on the porch they were building. Another young lady, estranged from her father for most of her life, had just reunited with him. They'd reconnected shortly before his death—she found comfort in that.

During my stint at Candler I faced some of the highest highs and lowest low. I've heard it said that the program is designed to break you down and build you up again—boy did I break down. In 2005, I had a significant bout with depression (and potential PTSD) due to the landfall of Hurricane Katrina—a

Category 5 hurricane that hit Florida and Louisiana, causing catastrophic damage, particularly in the city of New Orleans and the surrounding areas, and over 1,200 deaths. Much like the 9/11 terrorist attacks, the grand exposure and weight of this horrific tragedy gripped me and took me to a dark place. It's during this time that the depression and anxiety was at an all-time high. I walked in rooms with people and had panic attacks for no reason at all. Consequently, I stayed at home as much as possible. I was barely functional—at times I wanted to kill myself. I remember one day sitting with a butcher knife and shredding the blanket that covered me. I began to hate myself and was torn between my reality with depression and anxiety and my faith that Jesus is a healer. I was torn between taking my medications and participating in counseling and confessing that I was already healed. I spent a lot of time on and off of medications, in and out of counseling, and vacillating between faith and depression. I'm convinced that the only thing that saved me was ministry—an opportunity to focus outside of myself.

During this time, I had an opportunity to partner with two families at Bethesda. Both permitted me to journey with them through the end of life for their loved one. Andrew was a beautiful man. For a short while, I was able to see him almost daily at his place of work and he always greeted me with a smile. During this time, I was in a deep depression, engaging as little as possible with the outside world. Somehow Andrew always caught my attention and greeted me with a hearty smile; I responded in kind. Some days it would be the only time I smiled. When I learned that Andrew, who was taking care of his dear wife after her stroke, also had a stroke, I was devastated. I visited and prayed with Andrew, but I don't recall that he ever regained consciousness. But that didn't stop me from visiting and sitting with Carol.

I also had an opportunity to visit with Anthony. Anthony was a piece of work—a former hairdresser turned quadriplegic with very limited speech—as feisty as they come. I believe because of his condition, he was vulnerable to mistreatment by the staff. He gave me space to advocate for him with the nursing staff. His sister, Melinda, lived on the West Coast so I would FaceTime her so she could see Anthony. I enjoyed visiting with him and did so almost weekly for a few months. He brought a lot of perspective to my experience and desire to live life to its fullest.

Through this type of ministry, I found my way from altar worker, to minister, and ultimately armor bearer—providing a sacred source of strength—to Lady Reese. As a minister, I was selected by both Bishop Reese, Jr. and Bishop Reese, III to provide training to the minister's and leaders on outreach and evangelism. Most notably, I taught a 7-series course on "Becoming a Contagious Christian" to the ministers that evolved into a monthly adult bible class campaign.

Both my personal life and ministerial life converged on many occasions. On one special occasion, my job selected me to attend a conference on AIDS and the Church at Saddleback Church, Rick Warren's church in Lake Forest, California. The conference was amazing and in a chance instance, I met Pastor Elijah:

"Pastor Elijah grew up in extreme poverty in rural Uganda. As one of 38 children in a polygamous family, he slept on the ground without a blanket for most of his childhood and almost died from insect infestations as a result at the age of eight. He received his first pair of shoes at age 15 and at 18, for the first time in his life, felt the satisfaction of a full stomach."[23]

With a big smile and a booming voice, he raised his arms and said, "My sister, come to Uganda!" Little did I know that God would open a door for me to do so. It was Pastor Elijah's first visit to the US, and I was the first person he'd met. I wanted to go to Uganda but, as not to be completely naive, I needed to learn more. It turned out that he too was travelling to Atlanta following the conference to connect with his sponsor, Anna. Indeed, it was a divine encounter. When I returned home, I met Anna and visited with Pastor Elijah. Some months later, I was in Uganda as a speaker at the 1st Annual Women Empowerment Conference. From there, I led mission teams to Uganda annually for the Youth Ablaze International Conference, not only ministering to upwards of five thousand East African youth and young adults, but also pastors and leaders.

I must say, when I arrived it Uganda I felt as if I'd never lived. I was able to breathe as never before; the sun seemed so close it was as if it kissed the earth. Even as the people spoke Luganda, it seemed I understood the context and sentiment of their heart as if it was my native language. I learned the stories of many women—how they borrowed dresses and walked tens of hundreds of miles just to be in attendance. I'd never seen such a thirst for nor a move of God as this. The presence of God was palpable, and I immersed myself into every moment. The first year was particularly unique in that I had no idea what to expect as I ministered to thousands of women and girls. The churches filled until they overflowed, and the crowds then surrounded the edifice. I also met with and encouraged pastors like Pastor Margaret. I had an opportunity to sit in her home, hear her story, and impart encouragement. Some pastors lead the people without possessing a bible; others walk miles and miles to and from their congregants just to preach the Word. At the end of the day, much of what we have they are devoid of, yet they worship deeper, praise higher and give thanks despite their abject poverty. Having dealt with depression for several years, mission work turned out to be the balm that soothed all that ailed me. Mission work gave me purpose beyond measure and imposed a call to share the work with others. To think, from the girl next door with social anxiety to a minister to the nations. Only God could use me in my weakness.

Bethesda nurtured me, equipped me to quench my thirst for God, supported me in my call to ministry, encouraged me toward seminary, ordained me upon commencement, and ultimately, in partnership with God, sent me to the nations. Indeed, Bethesda matured me, taught me about myself, the value of relationship and community, the character and nature of God, and the work of the ministry. It has exposed and leveraged my best gifts to the glory of God. For this, and much more, I am enriched and eternally grateful. Indeed, I gave the ministry my guts (played full out) and received everything in return, including a husband.

In 2012, I met my husband Dave at Bethesda. We had crossed paths a few times, once when he expressed interest in a praise team mission trip; another time when he was working in the church bookstore and donated toward my churchwide fundraiser; and finally, at a community event. Follow the event, he invited me to the Navy Ball. This tall, handsome man, both shy and unassuming, proved to be a gentle giant. He picked me up in what appeared to be plain clothes, covering his uniform until we entered the event space. I asked him about his Clark Kent stunt, and he explained the modestly he assumes concerning his uniform. A leader in the Navy, he was humble and honorable beyond measure; every shipmate that I met at the ball spoke well of him from sportsmanship to mentorship. I, on the other hand, was a nervous wreck. I hadn't been on a date in what seemed like forever and I liked him—I really liked him. We went on a few dates and had a wonderful time. One day I called him and ask him what he was doing, his response was "preparing for our future." I knew he was sincere and simply allowed our fairy tale to unfold.

Dave, an amazing man, is a retired Navy and Marine veteran. We were engaged after six months of courtship and remained so for a year until we got married. I experienced a lot of anxiety during this time, but I employed two things to help me get through this period. First, I used an anxiety technique where you just say how you're feeling; you speak out the anxious thought as to overcome it. For example, if I'm afraid I may panic while having lunch with Dave, I'd simply say to him, "Coming into this situation I was afraid I may panic but I'm feeling much better now that we're together." Another technique I used I learned from Tony Robbins' conference Unleash the Power Within—he calls it playing full out. This was also encouraged by my success coach. So, if I wanted to call Dave, I called him—it didn't matter who called last or how long it had been. I wanted to be in a relationship. I wanted to find love. I wanted the fairy tale. And while there's been no magic involved and we've had our challenges, I got just what I wanted and needed. In 2014 on my birthday, we happily married. With the hope of a fresh start in ministry together, we transitioned to Kairos Empowerment Church immediately afterward.

Kairos, a small storefront church, put me in mind of Bibleway. It was a startup pastored by my dear, anointed friend Ramon. Pastor Ramon is highly gifted to preach and has a heart of gold. He and his wife, Lady Abigail, welcomed Dave and I with opened arms. Observing the two of them with one small child, and one on the way, was an inspiration to Dave and me. We felt afire and deeply desired to help build the church, but things didn't go as planned.

Serving at an established church like Bethesda and serving at startup church like Kairos was like night and day for me. Feelings of anxiety and uncertainty created the perfect storm. As a leader at Bethesda, I was accustomed to being scheduled and prepared to address the congregation. In contrast, as a leader at Kairos, a much smaller church, I was often put on the spot to address the people. Consequently, I was set on edge every time I entered the doors of the church. Through no fault of Pastor Ramon, I was uncomfortable and becoming increasingly detached and depressed, even lamenting my separation from Bethesda. In hindsight, I should have said something, but I didn't—my hope was to adjust.

Having travelled to Uganda with me in the past, Pastor Ramon was excited about the potential of missions ministry at Kairos and returning to Uganda. I planned a mission for us but, as Pastor Ramon was expecting his second child, he was unable to attend. Dave and I travelled alone, and while the ministry was rich, the trip paled in comparison to the prior year when we hosted a large team. It seemed everything around me was changing. For better or for worse? I'm not sure but it was different, and the change was hard.

The next year, now pregnant with Melody, I planned a mission trip to Cuba. It was an uneasy experience. For one, it was my first Spanish speaking mission and I felt some disconnect in understanding the people and the context therein; and secondly, the team didn't come together as I'd hoped—it seemed to have a life of its own. Perhaps I was overly sensitive and inflexible. Having participated in and led six consecutive missions, for me, missions had become a sacred spiritual practice that deserves the utmost respect. Not everyone on the team held that same perspective and it was pervasive. Feeling estranged—from the mission and the team—I slumped further into depression and made a point to set myself on the margins at Kairos. This was new for me. I was used to being present and accountable in ministry. I felt a break within my beloved community, and I couldn't shake it. I haven't been on the field since and miss missions dearly.

Starting a family also greatly affected my involvement in ministry. I rarely went to church. I didn't want to buy little clothes or decorate her room; rather, I was more concerned about what a baby would do to our marriage. The first year of marriage had not been easy but I loved our companionship and feared a baby would take away from the intimacy of just Dave and me. Dave on the other hand was excited about the thought of having a baby girl and the joy she would bring to our family. He was right. Melody changed our lives in the best way and brought a ton of joy and partnership that we'd never experienced yet I still found myself low. I missed her being in my tummy. I felt a weight and heaviness I'd not experienced before. During labor and delivery, I had some complications. My IV had to be replaced 9 times and my epidural was problematic. My blood pressure also began to rise. And although I was discharged, I was soon readmitted with severe preeclampsia.

This condition caused another combination of issues. For one, I was initially separated from my baby; two, I was in too much pain to breastfeed which compromised my milk supply. And finally, I was overwhelmed and exhausted beyond measure—the type of exhaustion that makes you want to do things... At times I not only wanted to kill myself but also my sweet Melody. I thought about jumping off our balcony or any high place for that matter, but no place seemed high enough—I was afraid to survive and live in the shame of attempted suicide. I also thought about dashing Melody's head on the ground, but I knew if I killed her, I would also have to kill myself. I was in a quandary and lost without ministry and a community of faith.

After about a year of untreated PPD, analyzing scenarios to end my life and rationalizing why they wouldn't work, I sought help through my primary care physician. She didn't refer me to a psychiatrist rather, she just prescribed me "Vitamin Z," her code for Zoloft. I was on Zoloft for a about a year. I don't recall any marked improvement but I felt the need to be responsible and accountable for my mental health, so I continued until I conceived again; despite being considered among a class of drugs that are safe to take during pregnancy, being high risk, I didn't want to chance it. Dave and I had been trying for a few months and were excited to conceive. But, in going to the doctor, a heartbeat could not be found. We were not too alarmed because we had a similar experience with Melody—the doctor advised that there was no heartbeat and recommended a dilation and curettage (D&C). We refused and on our next visit rejoiced at the sound of her beating heart. But this time it was different—there was a second and third doctor's visit and still no heartbeat.

Finally, my doctor confirmed a spontaneous abortion or miscarriage. I was given the option to allow the fetus to naturally evacuate or schedule a D&C. I scheduled a D&C but later that day, while getting my hair done, I began to feel contractions. Not sure what was happening, I went to the restroom and before I knew it, I had our unborn fetus into my hand. I was in shock for a moment. I wanted to preserve it somehow—to appropriately memorialize it but I was without recourse, so I flushed our unborn baby down the toilet and returned back under the hair dryer. I felt so helpless, cold-hearted, sad. From that experience, I don't think I'll ever be the same.

Despite attempting to treat bouts of depression and anxiety with faith and medication, in my experience, I found that where most doctors embraced and encouraged spiritual practice, most pastors discouraged the use of prescription medication in treating mental illness; and made light of mental institutions. I can't count the number of times faith over medication was preached or pronounced, necessitating, for me, an unhealthy relationship between faith and medicine, a conflict with prescription compliance.

*"She used to pick me up when I was down
She changed my whole life around
And I missed my,
missed my grandma,
my grandma,
my grandma's hands
And I missed my grandma,
my grandma,
my grandma's hands."*[24]

Two weeks after our miscarriage, my grandmother died. Thankfully, something about my grandma's life and death charged me to live again and I began to have hope. I decided to take control of my health and avail myself to others by enrolling in a health coach certification program. Thanks to Anana Harris Parris, author of *Self Care Matters: A Revolutionary's Approach*, I began to work my baby steps and see many improvements. I was nearing my goal weight, preparing for my headshots and then I found out that I was pregnant again. Though I was happy, at the same time, I was devastated because I'd finally come to a point where I was doing something for me, but I now had to again yield my body over to maternity. I've heard it said, watch what you pray for because you just might get it. I've also heard it said that we make plans and God laughs. All jokes aside, I was depressed throughout my entire pregnancy. I was afraid of having another miscarriage; alternatively, having a high-risk pregnancy, I was afraid that something may happen to me or the baby. Fortunately, I carried Malakai full-term and was induced as scheduled. He was a healthy, beautiful newborn.

My labor and delivery were uneventful, but I began to know and feel that my blood pressure was increasing both following delivery and discharge. Having experienced preeclampsia before, I knew what to expect. But when checked by the emergency room physician I was discharged. When I learned the news, I summoned the doctor and told him he was making a big mistake. It is a shared belief within the Black community that doctors do not always believe you when you are a Black woman; I have experienced this. I am also aware of the cultural mistrust of the health care system within the Black community; I too am guarded in navigating my health care. However, I have found that when I participate in and advocate for my mental health and well-being, I receive the best possible care. They held me for observation and ultimately found that I was indeed preeclamptic again. The most difficult part about preeclampsia is the initial separation from the baby and the added pain that comes with the condition. Due to dangerously elevated blood pressure, my symptoms included a deafening headache. Again, I was faced with a cocktail of issues-I was separated from my baby, I was in too much pain to breastfeed which compromised my milk supply, I was overwhelmed and exhausted! Oddly, this exhaustion did not come and go; rather, it seemed to deepen and become more treacherous. Again, I found myself in a place where I wanted to not only take my life but also my sweet Malakai. I fantasized about jumping... I considered dropping the baby... it was an awful time.

At six weeks postpartum, I went for a checkup and could do nothing but cry. Dr. Kurt Martinuzzi, having saved my life before, again saved my life. He gave me a quiz to assess if I was depressed and then confidently told me my score was terrible. He not only put me back on Zoloft but also stood by as I scheduled an appointment with a psychiatrist; he also called my husband to tell him that I was suffering with depression. This was not a good time for me, but I was wise enough to know that Dr. Martinuzzi was not being aggressive for show—he was protecting me from what happens when depression, postpartum or otherwise goes unchecked. I am forever grateful.

PART THREE

My Journey with Postpartum Depression

"Symptoms of some mental or physical illnesses or conditions can create difficulties in the building of the attachment, such as an inability to get out of bed, lapses in memory that the baby is even there, problems with understanding what the baby needs, barriers in getting to the baby, and issues that require frequent hospitalizations of or separations from the caregiver."[25]

"A mother has to reevaluate and integrate new information with each new baby."[26]

"Today she arrives 10 minutes late, in sweatpants, accompanied by her infant son. Her affect is somewhat dysphoric, constricted. She complains of difficulty functioning, not caring for self (bathing, cooking, feeding), losing track of time, not paying bills, grocery shopping is stressful, hasn't done laundry, her 3-year old's socks didn't match" (April 4, 2019).

As a follow-up to my interaction with Dr. Martinuzzi, I was evaluated at Emory Women's Mental Health Program by doctors Helania Jaffee and Toby Goldsmith. Doctor Jaffe, a resident at the time, was a thoughtful, cautious practitioner. She asked a lot of the right questions, listened intently and provided Dr. Goldsmith with an accurate assessment and thoughtful plan. On one occasion, Dr. Jaffee asked if I thought I could be a better mother to my children if I wasn't depressed. It was a revelatory question as I realized the toll my symptoms may be playing on my children, particularly Melody. Often, I found myself just handing over my phone rather than engaging her with a game, a book or simply a conversation. I was unconsciously distancing myself from Melody rather than being the mom I know I can be. Provided are some excerpts from my time with Dr. Jaffee:

Her mood is better, more calm, less hot tempered. Not "sad" but still very tired, exhausted, sleeping max 2-3 hours at a time due to baby's schedule, and feeling anxious, "overwhelmed." Has days of normal functioning, then 2-3 days not functioning at all (ordering food out, not showering, brushing teeth, or getting dressed). She hasn't opened mail in a month, has a lot of responsibilities, daughter is potty training. She is worried about lights getting shut off, daughter being troubled or getting made fun of, son going to daycare (recently refusing a bottle). Some nights she can't sleep while baby is sleeps, anticipating, feeling "wired" …continues losing weight" (April 25, 2019).

"She reports feeling "off," not herself, stressed, anxious,

agitated, short tempered. Per therapist, "Some days she is not getting out of bed, showering or dressing." Sleep is poor 4-5 hours per night, with delayed onset; appetite is poor, but she will occasionally binge. Started making progress, then got sick and had increased psychosocial stressors...she is having trouble engaging in family activities, does not want to see people" (May 30, 2019).

"Zoloft reduced "recovery time" after stressor to get out of bed after days not weeks, not sad or tearful, but still quite anxious; she has been more active, going out, encouraged by jenny; not sleeping all day, getting up to get daughter ready and just taking a morning nap now that husband is taking daughter to school. She sleeps well, but still breastfeeding every 2 hours" (June 20, 2019).

"She reports initial improvement in mood, bot back to self – lost 40 lbs. of baby weight by exercising (mixed martial arts daily), participating in IOP, sleeping better, functioning better...left program – has seen backslide since. Mood is more depressed, motivation is lower, has not been working out, eating more sweets, gained back 9 lbs., sleep is down to 3-4 hours per night. However, has not resumed sleeping all day, doing errands to prepare to return to work Monday. Worried about her word performance, being able to work the whole day. Denies suicidal ideation" (August 8, 2019).

Dr. Goldsmith was a feisty genius of sorts. She knew her stuff and hit the nail on the head with precision every time we engaged. Renowned for her work, Dr. Goldsmith knew how to get results and set me on a path for healing. Coupled with continuing the Zoloft and prescribing Abilify, she referred me to Jenny Barwick, a Licensed Professional Counselor with a private practice named Searching for Vitality, LLC; and collaborated with Jenny to get me enrolled in the Transitions Behavioral Health Programs, a part of Emory University Hospital at Wesley Woods.

Jenny, kind, gentle and very mellow, understood exactly where I was and provided great insight and guidance that proved to make the difference for me. What made her most approachable was the fact that she too had a toddler and graciously disclosed some of the challenges she faced following the birth of her son. I attended weekly counseling for months and, using a "variety of techniques, compassion, and nearly a decade of experience," Jenny helped me find the vitality I was looking for. Here are some of the things I could count on Jenny to say:

"It is ok to not be ok.

You are worthy of feeling better.

It's ok to need help and courageous to seek it out.

I look forward to helping you.

You are not alone.

You're a good mom."

Jenny invited me to share my story and together, we discovered what "ok" meant for me. She also provided me with several handouts and resources, including the "Motherwise Support Group" at the Atlanta Birth Center.

Motherwise Support Group is for pregnant and postpartum women. I participated in this free group because I didn't want to be feel alone. Like the other moms, I brought Malakai, listened and shared my story. At times I felt on the margins as I was the only mom who named and talked about PPD, but I found comfort in knowing that what I shared may help someone suffering in silence; and I found strength in owning my story. I also found strength in partnering with Pea Pod Nutrition and Lactation Support, also located at the Atlanta Birth Center. When Malakai was three months old, my husband went out of town for two weeks for Naval training. During this time, I had the novel idea to increase my breast milk supply by exclusively breast-feeding Malakai rather than supplementing with a bottle as that was typically Dave's role. However, when Dave returned, Malakai would no longer take a bottle from him—he wouldn't take a bottle at all! I struggled for three months to get him back on the bottle. Fortunately, I had the support of Founder and Executive Director of Pea Pod, Alicia Simpson and Catherine "Cat" Palmer, a lactation consultant. Both Cat and Alicia were full of passion and eager to help me and Malakai transition to a more workable feeding plan. More importantly, they helped me discover that Malakai had both a lip and tongue tie; and provided me with a resource to address the issue.

Despite a host of resources and support, at times, I still felt very alone and struggled with thoughts of suicide. While I never made plans to commit suicide, the intrusive thoughts disturbed me and propelled me to take aggressive strides toward my goal—to get better for my children—through counseling. In doing so, I gained confidence where it had diminished and learned to be gentler with myself. I also learned how to better engage Dave to solicit the help I needed. Through counseling I realized that I never really shared my struggles with depression with him; quite the contrary, I did everything I could to show Dave that I was ok. I found that I wasn't being honest with him but eventually found the courage to tell him that I wasn't ok; I wasn't managing, and I wasn't well. Jenny held some joint sessions with us and provided Dave with some resources as well; our marriage was better for it, but the depression took a toll, nevertheless.

Initially, the debilitating effects of depression were frustrating to Dave. He didn't understand and, on several occasions, told me to snap out of it. If only it were that easy; I couldn't snap out of it. My baby's needs and the needs of my family were immediate, but my recovery was slow; so, many times, Dave had to make up the difference. I, on the other hand, felt like Dave was demanding too much from me, I felt life was demanding too much—as a result, I may be in the bed up to five days at a time. For example, my husband's family, which is very large, holds an annual Easter party. It took everything in me to shower, get dressed, help with the kids, show up and engage. Consequently, I was bed ridden for four days. I'm naturally an introvert so being around others tends to drain me. When depressed, it drains me more. Its only when I can spend time alone or at least at home that I recharge. In considering what really helped me progress— it was not only the consistent support of my husband and mother but also my integrated health care team. One thing Jenny noted is that she didn't feel that Dave understood the seriousness of my condition—she was quick to explain that there was always potential for my condition to worsen which could be a detriment to both myself and the kids. Indeed, I didn't make it easy for Dave—my mood was up and down, and my emotions were set on edge. In her book The Postpartum Husband: Practical Solutions for Living with PPD by Karen Kleiman, Karen warns husbands, here's what you're up against:

"If you tell her you love her... she won't believe you.

If you tell her she's a good mother...she'll think you're just saying that to make her feel better.

If you tell her she's beautiful... she'll assume you're lying.

If you tell her not to worry about anything... she'll think you have no idea how bad she feels.

If you tell her you'll come home early to help her... she'll feel guilty.

If you tell her you have to work late... she'll think you don't care."

Then she says, but you can:

"Tell her you know she feels terrible.

Tell her she will get better.

Tell her she is doing all the right things to get better (therapy, medication, etc.).

Tell her she can still be a good mother and feel terrible.

Tell her it's okay to make mistakes; she doesn't have to do everything perfectly.

Tell her you know how hard she's working at this right now.

Tell her to let you know what she needs you to do to help.

Tell her you know she's doing the best she can.

Tell her you love her.

Tell her your baby will be fine."

On a positive note, there were many things I could count on Dave for. I could count on him to help around the house, throw in a load of laundry, pick-up take-out for dinner, educate himself about PPD through Jenny, to include emailing her with concerns and questions but most of all I could count on him to be patient with me.

Dave knew it was a struggle for me to get dressed and get to my appointment once a week with Malakai in tow, but he encouraged me, and Jenny made me feel comfortable. In her office was a changing pad, toys and she made known that she was nursing friendly. I often sat on the floor and changed or nursed Malakai. As time progressed, I got better but I remained concerned. Here's a letter that I wrote to Dr. Goldsmith regarding my recovery:

Hi Dr. Goldsmith,

As suggested, I am taking sertraline and working with Jenny Barwick. This treatment plan is helping however, I am anxious that my return to work date is approaching faster than my recovery is progressing. In addition, my infant, Malakai, is now a bottle refuser (my husband went away for a two-week Navy training about 45 days ago and my little one has refused a bottle ever since), which only compounds my anxiety around putting him in daycare.

I need more time to do the work of recovery, get my husband on board, and work with Malakai. I spoke with Jenny about this and believe she and I are on the same page; she advised that I reach out to you regarding this request in advance of my 5/30/19 appointment with you and Dr. Jaffe. Jenny will begin working with both my husband and I in June. In addition, I spoke with Christy at Breastfeeding Atlanta and plan set up a series of lactation consultations.

My short-term disability benefit runs through 6/17/19 however, I am eligible to extend my benefits through 8/17/19 with your endorsement. I request your assistance (paperwork attached).

Thank you, Laray

In collaboration, both Dr. Goldsmith and Jenny found that I would benefit from more immersive treatment. They referred me to Emory University Hospital at Wesley Woods. In this I found there were resources that I knew not of. Others were taking advantage of them. It was my turn.

Patient: Dyer, Laray Essence

Age: 41 years

Sex: Female

DOB: 4/12/1978

History of Present Illness

Laray Dyer is a 41-year-old Project Manager at the Centers for Disease Control and Prevention who presents to the Psychiatric Adult Intensive Outpatient Program (IOP) for management of depression characterized by fatigue, irritability, feeling "zombied out," evolving from tearful to anxious, irritable and irascible after starting Sertraline. She explains she had some depression after the birth of her three-year-old, and after the birth of her second baby, things got considerably worse. She recalls scoring "depressed" on a postpartum screening while at the hospital, and the problem escalating to the point that, six weeks out, she was having troubles with the basics, like bathing. She was struggling to get out of bed and worried about returning to work..." (Adult Intensive Outpatient Program Initial Evaluation, Emory University Hospital at Wesley Woods)

As Jenny talked with me about the Adult Intensive Outpatient Program (IOP), my initial response was fear and intimidation. I was afraid of the type of people I may hold space with and intimidated by the perceived severity of my own condition. Nevertheless, I was desperate for a breakthrough, so I consented to participate. During intake, I mentioned my fear of being surrounded by individuals with mental illness to Michael McDade, Intake/Referral Development Coordinator, and he simply said, "they're just like you." He was right—I discovered that I had a lot more in common with the participants of the program than I'd originally thought.[27]

Our care was individually managed by an interdisciplinary clinical team consisting of a nurse, psychiatrist, and psychotherapist. In addition, we met in a small group, seeking to learn effective coping and preventative awareness skills; topics included managing depression and anxiety, guilt and shame, crisis management, family dynamics, healthy relationships, community resources, healthy boundaries and coping with change. We learned, we listened, and we lamented; we were given space to process and explore real-life situations as they happen, and practice newly acquired healthy behavior skills.[28]

I remember sharing a story that brought me to tears. My hairdresser, who I thought of as a friend, significantly damaged my hair by applying severe tension and glue to a style that pulled out my edges, ageing me about 20 years. When I brought this to her attention, first she acted as if nothing was wrong with my hair. Then she tried to make it like I came to her with damaged hair. Finally, she agreed to treat my hair for damage at my expense. I was so distraught—not only because of my hair but also because I trusted her and considered her a friend; and rather than providing empathy and comfort I was met with confrontation. This experience felt symbolic of a pattern I've repeated where I upheld my role in the relationship, but the other party had no reservation with rejecting me and relinquishing their role which is distressing. But, with the support of the group I realized 1) my damaged hair was a temporary situation—it would grow back; and 2) it was good that I was distressed as it helped me to see a larger pathology at work. Indeed, learning new skills, listening to others and sharing my story was empowering.

I was immersed in this environment for several hours three times per week. It may not sound like a lot, but it was intense and served to undergird me in navigating my day-to-day recovery. It wasn't until I was discharged that I realized how much support IOP truly provided. I regressed a bit but took on the next challenge like a boss: I prepared to return to work.

"The term "neuropsychological evaluation" refers to a process whereby a qualified clinician, typically a licensed psychologist, collects information about their client from different sources, puts it all together, analyzes it, and determines if there are any neurological reasons why certain activities such as school, work, behavior, or maintaining social relationships, might be challenging."[29]

"In a very real sense we have two minds, one that thinks and one that feels."[30]

Despite the support I was receiving through IOP, I still was not at peace with the notion that I was simply suffering with PPD; rather, I felt there was a larger issue at work. My symptoms remained significant, and I was cloudy—having a hard time remembering much of anything. So, I asked Dr. Goldsmith to partner with me in obtaining a psychological evaluation. She connected me with Dr. Glen Eagen and within a couple weeks I was scheduled for testing.

I found Dr. Eagan to be a very pleasant man; kind, patient and passionate about drilling down to the right tests to help me get the answers I was searching for. Before I share the findings from his report, I must say that there are some interesting and controversial results that come to light. I don't agree with the report in its entirety, but I believe it's important to break the stigma around psychological evaluation; the purpose is simply to diagnose and treat mental illness. I insert this report as a form of resistance against the embarrassment that many who deal with depression, anxiety, and bipolar disorder experience; and to reveal what to expect when expecting a psychological evaluation. Despite being evaluated during a mental health crisis, I am not ashamed of the test results, treatment considerations nor conclusions. It is well with my soul.

Provided are the findings from his report:

August 7, 2019

Psychological Evaluation

Patient: Laray Essence Dyer

Date of Birth: April 12, 1978

Ms. Dyer was evaluated pursuant to a referral by Toby Goldsmith, M.D., that concerned her cognitive functioning.

Sources of information:

Interview and testing of the patient conducted by Dr. Glenn Egan at the Emory Clinic in August 1, 2019, for approximately three hours and 30 minutes; Ms. Dyer's Emory Clinic medical records.

Notification of referral:

At the outset of the evaluation, Ms. Dyer was informed of the referral and that the results of the evaluation would be presented to the psychiatric staff currently treating her. She was also told that her medical records would be reviewed as part of this evaluation. Ms. Dyer agreed to proceed with the evaluation.

Presenting problems:

Ms. Dyer stated that she has a history of depression and anxiety and wanted "insight into cognitive difficulty." When asked to rate the recent level of her emotions and a scale of 1 to 10, Ms. Dyer rated anxiety as a 7, depression as a 6, and irritability as an 8. She rated problems with hyperactivity as a 7 for the past two months and problems with attention/concentration as a 10 for the past three years but has been somewhat of a problem since an automobile accident in 2008. She also rated mood swings as a 7. She rated memory problems as a 10 for the past 3 years. When asked to rate how traumatic memories are affecting her, she rated it as a one.

Background:

Ms. Dyer is a 41-year-old right-handed, African American female who states that she was in a boarding school (the Milton Hershey School) from third grade until the seventh grade and "loved it." She then attended an all-White high school but did not feel accepted and went to an all-Black college but lacked friends there also. She later completed a Master's degree in public policy and management from Carnegie Mellon University and a Master of Divinity degree from Emory University. She reported no learning problems in school until she had a concussion from an automobile accident while in graduate school at Emory.

Ms. Dyer is currently employed by the Center for Disease Control (CDC) as a project manager but has been on extended maternity leave because of emotional problems following the birth of her son this spring. She said that she is scheduled to return to work in about a week. Ms. Dyer is married and lives with her husband and two children. She indicated that none of her blood relatives had been diagnosed as having dementia...

Ms. Dyer reported that she is five-feet, three-inches tall and weighs about 173 pounds. She indicated having a reasonably good appetite and said that she has lost about 40 pounds since joining an MMA Boot Camp about five weeks ago and continues to work out four to six times a week. She said that the exercise program helps her mood, prevents her from feeling sad, and makes her feel more connected to the outside world, and gets her more socially involved. However, she said that she gets an average of four hours of sleep and had only three hours of sleep the night before this evaluation. However, she stated that she does not have nightmares. When asked about her recreational activities she stated that she does "homemaking" in addition to her exercise program. She has her children in a daycare program and drives her car on a daily basis.

Ms. Dyer reported that her only significant head injury occurred in 2008 when she had a concussion as a result of an automobile accident. She believes that the accident may have caused some cognitive problems she has been experiencing but notices that those problems become "exacerbated since I've become depressed." She said that she had some psychological testing done at Emory's Wesley Woods but was told that the problems she was having were likely due to depression. She said that she does experience headaches but that they are moderate. She described her hearing as fair and her vision as good, without the need for glasses either for seeing at a distance or for reading. When asked about medical problems, she only reported having high blood pressure. She denied using any tobacco, alcohol, or recreational drugs. She also denied having any current legal problems.

Psychiatric Treatment:

When asked about her mental health history, Ms. Dyer reported never being hospitalized for psychiatric illness but that she did start receiving psychiatric/psychological treatment for anxiety and depression around 2008 while she was in graduate school at Emory. Ms. Dyer stated that she has never attempted suicide and denied having any [current] suicidal or homicidal ideation. She also said that she has not been concerned about anyone hurting her. She was unclear about whether she has experienced hallucinations or just perceptual illusions.

Ms. Dyer indicated that she has seen Dr. Goldsmith since the end of March 2019 and is receiving psychotherapy from Jenny Barwick, a licensed professional counselor who used to work for Emory but is now in private practice. She is now taking the following psychiatric medications at night: Zoloft (200 mg daily) and Abilify (10 mg daily). She indicated that she has never been treated with ECT.

When asked what was concerning her now, Ms. Dyer said that she was worried about going back to work. She said that she felt inadequate and was concerned that she was not able to do the work required of her. However, she said that she likes her boss, has earned raises, and has been complimented on her work. She also reported being under some stress trying to fix up a new home that she and her husband recently bought.

According to Emory Clinic medical records performed by Dr. Timothy Moore and dated July 18, 2019, Ms. Dyer is currently diagnosed as having a major depressive disorder, recurrent episode, moderate (F33.1). These medical records indicated that Ms. Dyer is currently prescribed sertraline 200 mg daily and aripiprazole 5 mg at night.

Behavioral Observations:

Ms. Dyer was alert, oriented, friendly, and cooperative with the evaluation. Her behavior was appropriate. Her speech was normal. And her eyesight and hearing appeared adequate for the evaluation. Her associations appeared logical. There was no behavioral evidence of hallucinations, delusions, or ideas of reference. Her mood was calm, and her affect was congruent.

Tests Administered:

Adult ADHD Self-report Scale (ASRS-v1.1) Symptom Checklist

Brief Cognitive Status Exam (BCSE)

Digit Span Test from the Wechsler Adult Intelligence Scale—IV (WAIS–IV)

Personality Assessment Inventory—(PAI)

Wechsler Abbreviated Scales of Intelligence—II (WASI-II)

Wechsler Memory Scale—IV (WMS-IV)

Test Results:

For comprehensive test results, see appendix E

Personality/Emotional Functioning:

The PAI is a 344-item self-report inventory in which a client is asked to rate each item as false, slightly true, mainly true, and very true. The test examines clients' experiences of factors such as anxiety, depression, problems thinking, substance abuse, suicidal feelings, and interpersonal behavior.

Validity of Test Results:

Ms. Dyer's scores suggest that she attended appropriately to item content and responded in a consistent fashion to similar items. The degree to which response styles may have affected or distorted the report of symptomatology on the inventory is also assessed. Certain of these indicators fall outside of the normal range, suggesting that Ms. Dyer may not have answered in a completely forthright manner; the nature of her responses might lead the evaluator to form a somewhat inaccurate impression of the client based upon the style of responding described below. With respect to positive impression management, there is no evidence to suggest that Ms. Dyer was generally motivated to portray herself as being relatively free of common shortcomings or minor faults. However, certain aspects of the profile raise the possibility of denial of problems with drinking or drug use, as individuals with similar personality characteristics typically report greater involvement with alcohol or drugs than was described by the client. Interpretive hypothesis in this report regarding the abuse of these substances should be viewed with caution. With respect to negative impression management, there is no evidence to suggest that Ms. Dyer was motivated to portray herself in a more negative or pathological light than the clinical picture would warrant.

Clinical Features:

The PAI clinical profile is marked by significant elevations across several scales, indicating a broad range of clinical features and increasing the possibility of multiple diagnosis. Profile patterns of this type are usually associated with marked distress and severe impairment in functioning. The configuration of the clinical scales suggests a person with significant thinking and concentration problems, accompanied by a heightened activity levels and irritable and expansive mood. Ms. Dyer is likely to be agitated and confused, feeling irritated with and estranged from people around her. Her social judgement is probably quite poor and these close relationships that have been maintained are probably strained by her moody and often demanding presence.

Ms. Dyer described significant problems frequently associated with aspects of a manic episode at a level of severity that is uncommon even in clinical samples. She is probably quite impulsive and unusually energetic, and most likely meets diagnostic criteria for a manic or hypomanic episode. She described an activity level that will be perceptibly high to most observers. She is probably involved in these activities in an overcommitted and disorganized manner, and she may experience her thought processes as being accelerated. Content of thought is likely marked by inflated self-esteem or grandiosity that may range from beliefs of having exceptionally high levels of common skills to delusional beliefs of having special and unique talents that will lead to fame and fortune. Her relationships with others are probably under stress due to her frustration with the inability or unwillingness of those around her to keep up with her plans and possibly unrealistic ideas. At its extreme, this irritability may result in accusations that significant others are attempting to thwart her plans for success and achievement.

A number of aspects of Ms. Dyer's self-description suggest noteworthy peculiarities in thinking and experience. She is likely to be a socially isolated individual who has few interpersonal relationships that could be described as close and warm. She may have limited social skills, with particular difficulty interpreting the normal nuances of interpersonal behavior that provide the meaning to personal relationships. Her social isolation and detachment may serve to decrease a sense of discomfort that interpersonal contact fosters. Her thought processes are likely to be marked by confusion, distractibility, and difficulty concentrating, and she may experience her thoughts as somehow blocked or disrupted. However, active psychotic symptoms such as hallucinations or delusions do not appear to be a prominent part of the clinical picture at this time.

Ms. Dyer demonstrates an unusual degree of concern about physical functioning and health matters and probable impairment arising from somatic symptoms. She is likely to report that her daily functioning has been compromised by numerous and varied physical problems. She feels that her health is not as good as that of her age peers and likely believes that her health problems are complex and difficult to treat successfully. Physical complaints are likely to focus on symptoms of distress in neurological and musculoskeletal systems, and may involve features often associated with conversion disorder, such as unusual sensory or motor dysfunction. She is likely to be continuously concerned with her health status and physical problems. Her social interactions and conversations tend to focus on health problems, and her self-image may be largely influenced by a belief that she is handicapped by her poor health.

Ms. Dyer reported a number of difficulties consistent with a significant depressive experience. The quality of Ms. Dyer's depression seems primarily marked by physiological features, such as a disturbance in sleep pattern, a decrease in level of energy, and a loss of appetite and/or weight. However, she does not seem to be reporting a significant degree of dysphoria or thoughts of worthlessness or hopelessness. This pattern suggests that she might not recognize the after mentioned symptoms as signs of dysphoria and stress or may be repressing the experience of unhappiness to some extent.

Ms. Dyer indicated that she is experiencing specific fears or anxiety surrounding some situations. The pattern of responses reveals that she is likely to display significant phobic symptoms and behaviors. These behaviors are likely to appear in some significant way in her life, and it is probable that she monitors her environment in a vigilant fashion to avoid contact with the feared object or situation. She is more likely to have multiple phobias or a more distressing phobia, such as agoraphobia, than to suffer from a simple phobia.

Ms. Dyer indicated that she is experiencing a discomforting level of anxiety and tension. The primary manifestations of Ms. Dyer's anxiety appear to be in the affective and physiological areas. Affectively, she feels a great deal of tension, has difficulty relaxing, and likely experiences fatigue as a result of high perceived stress. Overt physical signs of tension and stress, such as sweaty palms, trembling hands, complaints of irregular heartbeats, and shortness of breath are also present. In contrast, she does not report high levels of the cognitive symptoms of anxiety, such as excessive worry, negative expectancies, concentration problems, and diminished attention span.

Ms. Dyer described herself as rather moody and others may view her as overly sensitive. She may not be satisfied with her more important relationships and uncertain about major life goals. She also described herself as being more wary and sensitive in interpersonal relationships than the average adult. In addition, she reported a personality style that involves a degree of adventurousness, risk-taking, and a tendency to be rather impulsive.

Accordingly, to Ms. Dyer's self-report, she described NO significant problems in the following areas: antisocial behavior; problems with empathy. Also, she reported NO significant problems with alcohol or drug abuse or dependence.

Self-Concept:

The self-concept of Ms. Dyer appears to involve a generally positive but probably fluctuating self-evaluation. Her positive self-esteem may be a defense against feelings of uncertainty and self-doubt. Thus, the self-esteem is likely to be fragile and may drop dramatically in response to scrutiny or criticism by other people. Self-esteem may be maintained in such situations through attributing responsibility for setbacks to some external cause rather than to personal failings.

Interpersonal and Social Environment:

Ms. Dyer's interpersonal style seems best characterized as pragmatic and independent. She may tend to view relationships as a means to an end, rather than as a source of satisfaction. She is not likely to be perceived by others as a warm and friendly person, although she is not necessarily lacking in social skills and she can be reasonably effective in social interactions. Those who know her well are likely to see her as being shrewd, competitive, and self-confident.

In considering the social environment of Ms. Dyer with respect to perceived stressors and the availability of social support with which to deal with these stressors, her responses indicate that she is likely to be experiencing a mild degree of stress as a result of difficulties in some major life areas. She reported that she has a number of supportive relationships that may serve as a buffer against the effects of this stress. Ms. Dyer's current level of distress appears to be related to these situational stressors, and the relatively intact social support system is a favorable prognostic sign for future adjustment.

Treatment Considerations:

With respect to suicidal ideation, Ms. Dyer did report experience period and perhaps transient thoughts of self-harm. She is probably pessimistic and unhappy about her prospects for the future. Specific follow-up regarding the details of her suicidal thoughts and the potential for suicidal behavior is warranted. With respect to anger management, Ms. Dyer described her temper as within the normal range, and as fairly well-controlled without apparent difficulty.

Ms. Dyers interest in and motivation for treatment is typical of individuals being seen in a treatment setting, and she appears more motivated for treatment than adults who are not being seen in a therapeutic setting. Her responses suggest an acknowledgement of important problems and the perception of a need for help in dealing with these problems

Conclusions:

The results of psychological tests administered as part of this evaluation appear valid. She was cooperative with the evaluation and appeared to understand the directions. There was no evidence that a thought or mood disorder significantly interfered with Ms. Dyers ability to relate to me. The behaviors that Ms. Dyer exhibited during this evaluation were consistent with the observations recorded in her medical records.

Ms. Dyer's verbal and nonverbal reasoning ability as estimated by the WASI-II appears to be in the average range and possibly even in the high average range, which is consistent with her education and work history. She also performed exceptionally well on the digits forward subtest of the Digit Span Test, which indicated that she has the ability to do simple tasks that involve concentrating well. However, her lower scores on the digits backwards and sequencing sections of this test suggest that she struggles somewhat on tasks involving executive functioning. In addition, her perception that she is having difficulties with her memory is probably correct. Her memory performance, which varied between borderline and low average ranges, was also lower than expected. Although the test results provide no evidence for the likelihood of a major neurocognitive disorder, Ms. Dyer's memory performance may during this evaluation suggests that she may have difficulty functioning at work. The connection between executive functioning and memory functioning should be considered in light of her Personality Assessment Inventory test results, especially her significant scores related both to depression and mania. Although the relationship of her current cognitive issues to her head injury in 2008 is unclear, her memory functioning does appear to be hindered by problems in her emotional regulation.

Diagnostic Impressions:

F31.9 Bipolar Disorder

Recommendations:

Integrated psychiatric treatment and psychotherapy continue to appear needed.

In addition to a physical exercise program, Ms. Dyer should consider a program that would help her regulate her mood such as yoga or mindfulness training.

Cognitive and personality testing should be performed again in a year to identify how her cognitive abilities have changed in order to help clarify the diagnosis and treatment effects.

PART FOUR

Toward Mental / Emotional Health Care

"A self-care revolutionary is drowning in reasons, laced with habits, coated with people and surrounded by rules that do not support them taking good care of themselves anyway. It is not enough to be an activist, mother, father or leader who takes care of others. You must be a self-care revolutionary and fight to take care of yourself as well."[31]

Having and taking care of a baby is a delicate and difficult calling, especially during the first three months. Mom is healing from labor and delivery, adjusting to becoming a mother and operating on very little sleep; and baby is needy, acclimating to life outside of the womb. It's during this time that self-care is the most difficult and critically necessary.

In section two, I talked about my faith and ministerial journey during my first bout with PPD and leading up to my second. In section three, I talked about my experience with psychiatry and medication, psychotherapy and support groups, intensive outpatient therapy and psychological evaluation. Coupled, it was this strategic blend that brought me through PPD but not without one key element: self-care. Self-care is the number one thing you can do for yourself (and baby) to thrive.

For nearly two decades I battled with self-care, particularly in the area of assertiveness. I said "yes" to a fault. It's no wonder I found myself in frequent counseling and lacking a healthy sense of self. Taking caring of myself has always been hard for me and became less and less attainable as my responsibilities began to grow. It is my nature to take care of others first—to tend to work, ministerial duties, my children and my husband. So, taking caring of myself with PPD felt next to impossible. Nevertheless, if you desire to overcome PPD, self-care is essential. For the purpose of this section, I will focus on a few basic self-care elements that I struggled with and tried to employ on my journey through PPD.

Sleep hygiene is a critical component to self-care. PPD can lead to poor sleep quality, recent research shows. A new study shows that depression symptoms worsen in PPD patients when their quality of sleep declines. Sleep deprivation can hamper a mother's ability to care for her infant, as judgment and concentration decline.[32]

Having an infant and toddler makes it incredibly hard to get good sleep and early on I found myself breaking the cardinal rule— sleep when the baby sleeps! But something to do with trying to be a superwoman caused me to desire to "get things done" while the baby was asleep. On the other hand, even when I was tired, if I thought the baby would soon be waking, I would avoid sleep in anticipation. Finally, some nights I would just lie awake and observe my husband and infant sleep, as if I was on some type of watch. Consequently, the level of exhaustion I experienced literally made me want to kill myself; and I was severely irritable. In hindsight, I would better prioritize sleep, creating an environment conducive to sleep, as it has many benefits including reducing stress and improving your mood.[33] I would also investigate other ways to manage my stress.

Eating and taking medication, as prescribed, is also a critical component to self-care. At my lowest, I didn't eat and had no appetite. I lost all my baby weight rather quickly and then began to shed additional weight; I was losing weight every day. In all honesty, I could stand to lose some extra weight but doing so unhealthily was not safe, especially while breastfeeding. Eating three meals and two snacks a day helps keep energy levels up and protects your breastmilk supply, if nursing.[34]

According to Pfizer, to get maximum benefit from your medications, it is important to take them exactly as prescribed by your doctor.[35] During my low periods, I took less of my medication than prescribed or none. Lack of adherence to antidepressant medication can be a reason medications don't work, as well as a major barrier to depression treatment.[36] To support my compliance, I'd lean on my husband; if I was taking care of the baby and needed to take my medication, I would ask my husband to take over so I could take care of myself. When it's time to take medication, there's nothing more important.

Finally, as Jenny advised me, be kind to yourself, and keep your baby safe. According to Karen Kleinman, good moms have scary thoughts:

"Scary thoughts erupt without warning and terrorize this

sacred space between new mother and her baby. It's no wonder mothers have been reluctant to disclose these thoughts, even to loved ones, leaving them to collapse alone in disgrace with no safe place to fall."[37]

I can't count the number of times I had scary thoughts about hurting myself and my babies. Being a mom isn't easy and can sometimes feel insurmountable. Challenging thoughts may come and go but you always have the choice to acknowledge the thought and then extend compassion toward yourself; be kind to yourself and take care of your baby.

"This approach is not about acquiring more self-discipline or willpower. It's about personally discovering what nourishes you, what feeds you, and ultimately what makes your life extraordinary"[38]

While basic self-care is essential, enhanced self-care is the goal. Enhanced self-care is progressive—it's anything above and beyond nutrition, rest and maintaining the safety of those in the home. In an enhanced state, some days I'm doing well just to get up, wash my face and brush my teeth. Other days, I'm up for more of what will ensure that I'm taking care of me.

When suffering with PPD some of the most basic functioning is too difficult to perform. Early on, I found it extremely difficult to get out of bed; and most days, I didn't. I also found it difficult to maintain my personal hygiene. In hindsight, I believe the failure to take baby steps to get out of the bed prolonged my depression. I also think my refusal to keep up my personal hygiene was a passive-aggressive was of saying "I'm over it!" Alternatively, I could have strived to get out of bed by noon—giving myself an opportunity to sleep in until after the baby's first nap—even if that simply meant going downstairs to sit on the couch.

I remember sleeping over my grandma's house as a child and waking up to the smell of breakfast. Before I could get to the bottom of the steps good, she would shout from the kitchen "don't come down here without washing your face and brushing your teeth." Who would have thought that I'd still need to hear that as an adult? Now, I take on getting up and maintaining personal hygiene as an act of resistance against depression. Consequently, when it gets hard—when I don't want to get up or brush my teeth—it's a sign that I'm beginning to sink so I try and do it anyway.

When I'm up for more of what will ensure that I'm taking care of me, I reference my Institute for Integrative Nutrition Daily Journal for ideas. Within the journal is the following self-care checklist:

Morning intentions

Home-cooked food

Mindful eating

Tongue scraper

Hot towel scrub

Hot water bottle

Conscious breathing

Fresh air

Physical activity

Prayer/meditation

Meaningful connections

Touch/massage

Laughter

Time to myself

Visualized my future

I select at least one and indulge.

In addition, I reference Anana Harris Parris' book, "Self-Care Matters: A Revolutionary's Approach." In this text, she brilliantly decomposes self-care into the following categories and shares why this approach is revolutionary:

Spiritual & Emotional

Economic

Artistic

Physical

Educational

Social

I assess which area addresses my critical need and indulge accordingly. More specifically, Anana guides the reader on how to develop a self-care plan and encourages the reader to set goals and take baby steps therein. "The sweetest most revolutionary self-care step anyone can take is the first one. Take it over and over and over again."[39]

This past summer, I set a goal to become more physically active, so I joined a 6-week challenge at Independent MMA and Fitness. During this time, I mainly practiced boxing and kickboxing. I pushed myself, clawing my way out of depression, and obtained results. As I'm unable to maintain my membership now that I've returned to work, I set a new goal and opened two gym memberships—24-hour Fitness for convenience and LA Fitness for access to the pool. My baby step in this moment is to visit each one once per week. I soon will work up to a greater frequency to improve my health and lose weight.

"Out came the sun

And dried up all the rain;

And the itsy-bitsy spider

Climbed up the spout again."[40]

"Behold, I will do a new thing; now it shall spring forth; shall ye not know it? I will even make a way in the wilderness, and rivers in the desert. The beast of the field shall honor me, the dragons and the owls: because I give waters in the wilderness, and rivers in the desert, to give drink to my people, my chosen. This people have I formed for myself; they shall shew forth my praise."
(Isaiah 43:19-2, KJV)

As I complete this book, I don't have to reflect to remember what it feels like to suffer with PPD. I am yet suffering; that is, I still have moments where I feel my head is under water and need to take mental health days off but I'm surviving. I know and understand the signs, symptoms and manifestations of PPD; and the root of the depression and anxiety I've experienced most of my life. I also know and understand that instances of rejection serve to trigger feelings from my first life-defining moment. Nevertheless, I am no longer beholden to PPD, depression and anxiety, nor my past. I am healing.

The Lord declares, "I will do a new thing" and I feel that in my being. Even now, all things become new and I'm ready to transition from surviving to thriving. Dave and I are seeking a new faith community—we have visited several churches and have narrowed our search down to two promising communities. I am confident that this milestone will ground us in every self-care category—spiritual & emotional, economic, artistic, physical, educational and social.[41] To underscore this grounding, I've been invited to participate in a closed self-care support group; this is a rich opportunity to impart and glean from sisters holistically and I'm excited about it. "Call it a clan, call it a network, call it a tribe, call it a family. Whatever you call it, whoever you are, you need one" (Jane Howard).

I have a new psychiatrist (I'm still on medication) and continue to see Jenny. I also plan to follow-up with Dr. Egan—not only to discuss the results of my initial psychological examination report but also to schedule a follow-up evaluation for comparison. In the meantime, I plan to explore the potential of a type 2 bi-polar disorder diagnosis by educating myself on the disease.

My children are healthy and happy. My husband is a joy and finds satisfaction in our marriage and family; and I am well. As the saying goes, we may not have it all together but together we have it all.

"And I've learned that we must look inside our hearts to find

A world full of love like yours and mine

Like home."[42]

LARAY E. DYER

"If you think you might be suffering from any kind of postpartum mood disorder or are aware of some preexisting conditions in your life that could lead to it, DO NOT WASTE TIME! Get help right away."[43]

APPENDIX A:

THE UNTOLD STORY OF THE LATE STANLEE A. HOLBROOK

My wonderful sister, Stanlee, was a mother, a daughter, and a wonderful friend. To me and everyone who knew her best, she was also known as Boo Boo. She was always adventurous, spontaneous, and very outgoing.

Boo had a smile to light up a room. Boo was always wanting to save the world. Ever since we were children she was always wanting to help. She was called of God at the age of 5. She had a strong powerful voice; always walking around singing in and out of church. Stanlee had many talents growing up.

She started working at the very young age of 14. She was very wise and was preparing for the future. She was set to follow in my father's footsteps and go to Geneva College. She was a hard-working teenage student. She worked so hard that she worked her way to a manager position at the age of 15. Stanlee was always very popular and known for her style. Stanlee loved Jordan's and jewelry. She worked hard to pay for the things she liked and wanted.

When she was 16, she became an auntie. Sincere was the light of her world—nothing could separate the two. She reserved a lot of time before school and after, always wanting to be with him. No one couldn't tell her that wasn't her baby.

Coming into her teenage years, she began doing teenage things like going to parties and hanging out with friends. She also began to talk to an old friend from school named Jesse. They used to spend hours staying up late on the phone; and going on dates to the movies. Jesse used to pop up at her job to surprise her.

One day they had a bad falling out and stopped speaking to one another. Shortly thereafter, Stanlee found out she was pregnant. Now, a 17-year-old, teen mother, Stanlee was more motivated than ever to finish school, and work harder to give her child the world. She got a second job. Now pregnant, working two jobs, and going to school, she was very much dedicated to giving her son everything she could. Despite the odds, my sister had a stress-free pregnancy because family was there every step of the way, awaiting beautiful baby Lissayan.

I'll never forget when Stanlee went into labor. She had so many false alarms. One day, my mom and I knowing she was in labor, she thought she had a virus. My sister was walking around pacing the floor and then she finally screamed, "I can't take it anymore!" My mom laughed and said, "Those were the words I've been waiting to hear." That night a beautiful, chocolate baby was be born. Stanlee reached out to Jesse soon after giving birth and his family welcomed Lissayan with open arms.

Lissayan would change Stanlee's world. She graduated from high school and applied for her own place. Stanlee also enrolled into Geneva college but, always wanting to work, she left college to become a certified nursing assistant. She again graduated and began working.

I always admired my sister for applying herself to work hard and save; to take care of her son—she always wanted the best for him. She was living in her house, she had a new boyfriend, David, and she would celebrate Lissayan's first birthday. David and Stanlee were a young happy couple but soon would break apart. Nevertheless, they remained good friends. It was impossible for anyone to stay mad at Stanlee. Sadly, David would find himself in a tough situation—he ended up in a high-speed chase that ultimately took his life.

One short month later, we were awakened by the most disturbing call—that Jesse, Lissayan's father, was shot. He would survive for 12 days before succumbing to his injuries. The death of her only child's father would be a pain that I nor anyone else could understand. I watched my sister struggle with two back to back losses of people that she deeply cared for and it changed her life and the lives of those around her forever.

Temporarily moving in with my mom was a struggle for my sister; and every day she fought to be the same strong mother and now father she would have to be for her son. I was always there; we were never too far apart, spending everyday together. I still would never know the pain she felt. I wish I could take it all away.

Later, she would move into a new place and continue to raise her son with love, to be a light everywhere he went. Within one year later we would again be faced with death at her front door. Stanlee always wanted to help and open her door to anyone in need—family or friend. She had a family member staying with her. Sadly, our cousin would walk out of the building and be shot dead.

Soon after our young cousins' death, Stanlee was blessed with great news after a troubling year. She would find herself pregnant with a beautiful baby girl named June. June would be the joy she needed to give her the motivation she had been missing. Stanlee would find herself working again. My sister had a great bond with her family and most importantly all of her nephews and her nieces. My sister always wanted to party with the kids making sure every holiday would be extremely fun. Holidays would always be her favorite of all.

Even though she was always helping others my sister still struggled with an emptiness inside from losing Jesse. She sought out help in therapy. She also tried to self-medicate by smoking weed. She realized it was a problem and she would put herself in therapy for grief and for smoking. Nothing would bring her comfort. Watching her pain, I wish I could take it all away. There would be nothing I could do for her but be there for her whenever she called.

My sister and I, although our bond was so strong, would argue. But no matter what we would always be there for one another. No matter the time of day or night. Because of my love for my sister, I wanted to be there for her in every way. She had a hard time getting support for her daughter June. The father was denying paternity and responsibility for his child. It would become so stressful she would cry many nights not having one father for her children on this earth. One dead; the other just neglecting to help.

She, my mother, and I were always close. AS a result, she decided to move closer to mom so she could get more help now having three children--the youngest being in the hospital (Marionna Faith). Marionna was born with Laryngomalacia. This is another struggle that Stanlee would face as a young mother. My mother and I doing all could to help out with Marionna and the children; even taking turns staying at the hospital. After 6 long months, Marionna was released to come her to her mom and siblings, which included coming home on oxygen with strict instructions and series of important appointments. The battle was not over.

My sister was always on top of her game with her children always making sure they got what they needed and were where they needed to be. Nevertheless, we soon would see a shift in my sister attitude. My sister started acting different--talking to herself and just acting out of character. We all could see it and we suggested she talk to someone. She went to the hospital to take a little break. She would be there for at least two weeks. That would be a month before her death. She would come home of course, and she seemed to be doing fine but things would change, and it wasn't for the better.

I vowed to sit with her everyday no matter how good or bad. We did go to a business event I had and pride. We also took the kids to the arts festival, eating funnel cake and listening to music. Our favorite things to do around that time of the year was going out to eating in the middle of the day while the children were in school; going to Walmart and riding in handicap carts late night; and joking around being our naturally simple, goofy selves. Who would know these would be the last days I would spend with my sister my only sister?

Days before her death, on June 9th, we went to church. This would be our last service we attended together—something we have been doing together since we were little girls. In her words, it was the best service she had been to in a long time. She would leave that service with a heart-warming smile I haven't seen for a long time. On June 10th, we would wake up and have our usual daily phone calls and she would come down and get ready to go down to the art festival. On June 11th, I didn't hear from her—I would reach out but get no answer. Later in that day, I got a call from my dad that she was in Tennessee doing God's work saving lives! Not knowing what that work would be, I talked to my sister all day and night until she returned home on June 12th at 4:00 am. That day, I had court, so I didn't speak to my sister anymore. She decided to stay home and rest, later that day going to my mom's house.

The next day, June 13th, was the last day I would see or speak to my sister. She had called me for our usual morning conversation, and we decided to go to lunch with "the crew," as we called ourselves. We found ourselves at the movies instead. We saw Pokémon, the kids favorite. We bought 3D movie tickets with the glasses. The funniest thing would happen—we would sit with our glasses on thinking it was 3D only to find out it wasn't. We laughed about it later. After the movies we went to Starbucks and returned home. She dropped my children and I off at my house. She returned to my mom's house, as she did daily that being her home as she called it.

The next day I would never forget. I went out to eat with our dad for an early Father's Day gift and returned home, taking a nap with my son. I woke up to an urgent call to come to Children's Hospital. I walked into that hospital with chills I have never had before. My mom would greet me with news that my sister had jumped off a bridge.

My sister's life was love—she fought for love every day. Her children were everything to her. Her family meant the world to her. Depression from death is what took hold of my sister, no matter how hard she tried to escape it. Many people would think that my sister was alone. She was never alone—we talked, and she spent every day with my mother and me. She had a family that cared and loved her deeply. Not to mention Stanlee had a gang of friends. I strongly believe that my sister is at peace. If you read this and learn anything from my sister's struggle, she would say she fought, she even tried to come back across, but she slipped and fell. She never gave up.

Although it was her time, she wanted to save lives. So, I hope her story touches and reaches hearts all across the world. Even though she may have left her earthly body, her spirit lives on in her children, who she gave her best to everyday she woke up. She tried for Lissayan, June, and Marionna. I wish she could see Marionna now—she is walking and starting to talk.

We all miss you dearly and wish you would have stayed a little while longer! - *Your loving sister, Janet*

APPENDIX B:

POSTPARTUM DEPRESSION STORIES

Kholiwe Dlamini

There is always a certain level of anxiety when venturing into the unknown and I think that is normal. I knew my "anxiety" was not normal when it turned into constant crying and sadness. I avoided people as much as I could; I made excuses why I was unable to meet up with friends or family who wanted to see the new addition. Those that ignored the excuses and came to see the new baby were greeted with excuses and apologies for my appearance.

I love my children, but this journey called motherhood hasn't been anything like I imagined or planned. There is a lot of self-doubt, insecurities and tears. I thought I was alone, so I did what many do; I wore my mask. I smiled and participated in this thing called life as expected (I still do) because society expects me to "stay strong for my babies." No one ever spoke to me about postpartum depression all I knew about it was what I read on the form in the doctors' office. I always checked "no" I don't have postpartum depression because I did not want to be labeled or at worst have my babies taken away, so I thought.

The way I was raised, depression was not a thing so like all mental health issues I swept it under the rug and whaled every night while my husband slept peacefully next to me. Many nights I would beg God to take these feelings away until I got used to it as my new normal. "It's life." One deals with it, right?!

LuShaun Falconer

I am a work in progress. I have my moments when I feel sad and defeated, but I always seem to bounce back with resilience despite the odds. In addition to posting encouraging scriptures in my home, car and at my desk at work, my strong faith in God has been my greatest source of strength. Keeping my mind busy thinking positive frees me of the debilitating thoughts of doubt, fear, and anxiety. Safeguarding my emotional health with these self-care practices reduces my stress and supports my well-being.

Life events have been my main triggers of depression: marriage, stress at work, and postpartum. However, I am the real problem. Learning to do what I can and leave the rest up to God is not always easy, but it is necessary. My behavioral health issue has been very hard to accept. In my community, mental illness is seen as a "weakness" or you were labeled. Taught to be strong, trust in God, and pray away this diagnosis contradicted everything I knew.

I have concluded that I must do what works best for me. Yearly hospital visits are not an option. Although I struggle with my diagnosis it has caused me to work towards a stable lifestyle. I have accepted that treatment is vital in maintaining my life with family and friends. I now see a physician periodically to address my healthcare needs. I will never allow mental health to defeat me. Instead, I will continue to work towards being an advocate by breaking the barriers of this illness and demonstrating that you can be an overcomer.

Maureen Dyer

At the time when I was having babies PPD was not yet

recognized as a diagnosis biologically or physiologically. The term "baby blues" was used lightly with the expectation of the individual "getting over it soon".

My feelings of extreme sadness, crazy headaches, feelings of insecurity and failings would be looked at lightly and with a "poor dear, you'll feel better soon" attitude. Seeing we had no insurance, or money, to frequent the doctors; I had to "bite the bullet" and survive. Many days I did not want to move but the responsibility to the humans I brought forth every two years, fear of criticism from elders, coupled by no positive support from my life-partner or family forced me up and doing with some assistance from a beautiful sister-in-law (youngster) who shared in the sadness.

My savior was busyness: I taught school in the daytime and church work (not desk but physical operations) almost every night along with household and child-care duties forced me to operate with, and at times forget, the heaviness.

One year, ONE elderly Mother of the church saw my plight and without wordings from me, gave me some instructions that assisted me physically but the easily triggered mental sadness, feelings of defeat, tears inside and out and unrelenting headaches went on for years and years.

With a forceful need to feel and do better, spiritual involvements, helping others, prayerful heart and the success of my children I was brought to a point of healing.

Today I can say "I fought a good fight". Thank God for the strength to have persevered.

Anana Harris Parris

I told them I could still feel. No one believed me. The doctors proceeded to cut me open for a c-section anyway. I tried to jump off the table. They held me down, both shoulders, 10 months big, both legs and they kept cutting. I felt someone's hands wrenching around my insides, trying to get him out. I could feel everything.

I screamed. I fought. They pulled. Then a powerful drug entered my body and I blacked out. I woke up during surgery to the nurses and doctors sewing me up and talking about a movie they wanted to see. I didn't feel a thing, but I could hear them, and my belly was flatter.

I am sharing this beginning of my journey because my postpartum experience began as a post traumatic experience as well. I went home to no grandmother or doula. I went home to staples in my stomach and a looming infection. I went home to a working husband and the worst sense of depression and lack of hope I had ever felt. I wasn't prepared. Not only did I not want to live, I knew I didn't have what it took to care for this little person. Were it not for specific self-care strategies and my moment to moment choice to live, I would not be here.

It has taken years for me to shake that fresh feeling of hopelessness. It has taken me years to return to a dance class only to feel the pull of scar tissue and frustration. To say I quietly hid the emotional scars of postpartum depression for many years after my son's birth would be an understatement. No one seemed to care because so many women gave birth. Not until I started to care about me, about living, did my mind and thoughts get better. My story of postpartum depression is filled with darkness, embarrassment, and a lack of faith. My story of postpartum reminds me that I deserve compassion, kindness, and a grandmother's love hugging me the way I hugged my child. I can't even retell this story without crying. Such a horrible time that proved I truly want to live because I survived, not just a traumatic delivery, but I survived postpartum depression.

Chanel E. Martin

I had all my babies in entrepreneurship. That means there was no postpartum care, FMLA, time off, etc. With my first child, I was in the early stages of building—so if I didn't work, our company was greatly affected. The birth of my oldest was traumatic. She had to be sent to NICU, I suffered 3rd-degree lacerations, and we stayed in the hospital for nearly six days. Despite all the trauma done to my body, I only took about 2-3 weeks off for recovery. By four weeks, I was working again, and by five weeks I was traveling. Although I was not forced to go back to work, I didn't feel as though I could take a break. This greatly affected my mental health and the overall health of my family. Finally, pregnant with my fourth child, I see the need for rest and restoration.

De'Anna Janel Reaves

I lost my daughter 20 years ago on March 08, 2000 due to domestic violence in my marriage. My husband cut my throat and then proceeded to push me down the stairs and left me there for I don't know how long. He then returned and dropped me off at the hospital. When I woke up I had given birth to my daughter who only lived for 3 hours and 18 minutes. Even though it's been 20 years, I still suffer daily and the only thing that comforts me is God!! I've been through counseling in and out of church, but only God comforts and keeps me.

APPENDIX C:

ATLANTA BASED RESOURCES

Searching for Vitality Counseling Services

Perinatal Mental Health and Older Adult Mental Health

Jenny Barwick

(678) 343-5308

jsbarwicklpc@gmail.com

http://searchingforvitality.com/

Transitions Outpatient Behavioral Health Program

Adult Intensive Outpatient Program (IOP)

(404) 728-4776

https://www.emoryhealthcare.org/centers-programs/transitions-outpatient-program

Emory Women's Mental Health Program (WMHP) Clinical Care (Psychiatry)

Dr. Toby Goldsmith

(404) 778-5526

http://womensmentalhealth.emory.edu

Atlanta Birth Center

Midwifery/Gynecology, Prenatal Care, Postpartum Care, Women's Primary Care Services, Birth Services including water births, Women's Support Groups

(404) 474-2770

https://atlantabirthcenter.org/about/services/

PeaPod Nutrition & Lactation Support

Breastfeeding Education & Support, Nutrition Services, Pediatric & Adolescence, Women's Health & Prenatal, Classes & Workshops

Alicia C. Simpson

(678) 607-6052

info@peapodnutrition.org

http://peapodnutrition.org

Emory Brain Health Center

Psychological Evaluation

Glenn Egan, PhD

(404) 727-1483

http://www.emoryhealthcare.org/brain-health/conditions

Emory Clinic at 1365 Clifton Road

Obstetrics and Gynecology

Dr. Kurt Martinuzzi

(404) 778-7777

https://www.emoryhealthcare.org/emory-clinic/gynecology-obstetrics

APPENDIX D:

NATION-WIDE RESOURCES

National Suicide Prevention Life line : 1-800-273-8255

Suicide Prevention Hotline : 1-800-SUICIDE

National Postpartum Depression Warmline: 1-800-PPD-MOMS

https://www.2020mom.org/

MGH Center for Women's Mental Health

https://womensmentalhealth.org/

Postpartum Men

http://postpartummen.com/

Postpartum Progress

https://postpartumprogress.com/

Postpartum Support International

https://www.postpartum.net/

APPENDIX E:

PSYCHOLOGICAL TEST RESULTS

General Intellectual Functioning:

The Brief Cognitive Status Exam (BCSE) examines seven different areas of intellectual functioning: orientation, time estimation, mental control, clock drawing, incidental recall, inhibition and verbal production. The BCSE has five classification levels: Average, Low Average, Borderline, Low and Very Low. Ms. Dyer's overall score was 54 out of 58, which placed her overall cognitive functioning in the Low Average classification level for a person of her age and education. This classification represents 10-24% of cases within her age and education group and is not typically associated with global impairments in cognitive functioning. However, the item answered incorrectly that dropped her score into the low average range was getting the date wrong and was only missed by one day.

Attention and Working Memory:

The Adult ADHD Self-report Scale (ASRS-v1.1) Symptom Checklist is a questionnaire consisting of the 18 DSM-IV-TR criteria used to help identify an Attention Deficit Disorder. The first six of the 18 questions (Part A) were found to be the most predictive of symptoms consistent with ADHD. Part B contains the

WHEN THE BOUGH BREAKS

remaining twelve questions. The ASRS uses a five-point scale with the rating ranging from "Never" to "Very Often." On Part A, Ms. Dyer marked four out of the six items at a frequency that is constant with attentional problems but not with hyperactivity. On Part B which has 12 items, she marked four at a frequency consistent with attentional problems and five items at a frequency consistent with hyperactivity.

On the Digit Span Test, a client is first asked to repeat a series of numbers in the same order they were told, then asked to repeat a series of number backward, and finally asked to put a series of numbers in numerical order. The Digits Forwards score is useful as an indicator of the person's concentration/attention. The Digits Backwards and Digits Sequencing scores are useful as indicators of the person's working memory (ability to perform operations on short pieces of information held in memory) as well as attention. On this test, Ms. Dyer's performance for a person in that age group was as follows:

Digits	Raw	Scaled Score	Percentile
Forwards	14	14	91
Backwards	8	9	37
Sequencing	8	9	37
Total	30	11	66

Memory Functioning:

The WMS-IV is a test of verbal and nonverbal memory. The following is a summary of how Ms. Dyer performed on the primary memory indexes: (Index scores have a mean of 100 and a standard deviation of 15.)

Primary Indexes	Index Score	Percentile	95% Confidence Interval	Qualitative Description
Auditory Memory	83	13	77-91	Low Average
Visual Memory	75	5	70-83	Borderline
Immediate Memory	78	7	73-85	Borderline
Delayed Memory	087	19	82-92	Low Average

Ms. Dyer's primary subtest results were as follows:

Subtest Score	Scaled Score	Percentile
Logical Memory I	6	9
Logical Memory II	7	16
Verbal Paired Associates I	6	9
Verbal Paired Associates II	6	9
Visual Reproduction I	10	50
Visual Reproduction II	5	5

Ms. Dyer was also administered the WMS-IV Recognition subtests associated with the above free-recall memory subtests. Her cumulative percentage (base rate) was between the 26th and 50th percentiles on the Logical Memory II Recognition, was between the 10th and 16th percentiles on the Verbal Paired Associates II Recognition and was between the 17th and 25th percentiles on the Visual Reproduction II Recognition subtests

ABOUT THE AUTHOR

LARAY E. DYER

Laray is a highly acclaimed consultant, missionary and coach. She has fourteen years' experience providing diversified business and technology services and solutions to advance the mission of agencies such as the Centers for Disease Control and Prevention, Central Intelligence Agency, U.S. Navy, U.S. Army and U.S. Air Force Reserve. Laray has a passion for connecting with people through foreign missions, community outreach, and evangelism; and a gift for equipping and empowering pastors and leaders to fulfill their purpose. She holds a Master of

Divinity degree from Emory University and a Master of Science degree from Carnegie Mellon University; a Project Management Professional certification with the Project Management Institute and a Health Coach Certification with the Institute for Integrative Nutrition. Laray is a happily married mother of two residing in Atlanta, Georgia. For more information, check out her website at larayedyer.com.

BIBLIOGRAPHY

Black, K. (1996). A Healing Homiletic: Preaching and Disability. Nashville, TN: Abingdon Press.

Coleman, M. A. (2016). Bi-polar faith: A Black woman's journey with depression and faith. Minneapolis, MN: Fortress Press.

Harris Parris, A. (2017). Self care matters: A revolutionary's approach (K. Brundidge, Ed.). United States of America: YBF Publishing, LLC.

Shields, B. (2005). Down came the rain: My journey through postpartum depression. New York, NY: Hyperion.

Solchany, J. E. (2001). Promoting Maternal Mental Health During Pregnancy: Theory, Practice & Intervention. Seattle, WA: NCAST-AVENUW.

Townes, E. M. (2006). Breaking the Fine Rain of Death: African American Health Issues and a Womanist Ethic of Care. Eugene, OR: Wipf and Stock Publishers.

Endnotes

1   North, Arthur Walbridge (1910). Camp and Camino in Lower California. New York: The Baker & Taylor Company.

2   North, Arthur Walbridge (1910). Camp and Camino in Lower California. New York: The Baker & Taylor Company.

3   Solchany, J. E. (2001). Promoting maternal mental health during pregnancy: theory, practice & intervention. Seattle, WA: NCAST-AVENUW.

4   Ross, D. (1978). Track 23.

5   National Fatherhood Initiative. (2016). Father absence + involvement I statistics. Retrieved from https://www.fatherhood.org/fatherhood-data-statistics

6   Mission and sacred values. (2020). Retrieved March 29, 2020, from https://www.mhskids.org/about/ school-leadership/mission-sacred-values/.

7   Ross, D. (1978). Track 23.

8   Stacie, M. A. (2012). Unwritten rules. Las Vegas, NV: The Writer's Coffee Shop.

9   Harpo Productions, Inc. (2019). The 7 "uns" of daddyless daughters. Retrieved from http://www.oprah.com/oprahs-lifeclass/the-7-uns-of-daddyless-daughters-video#ixzz61U8hXegu

10   Williams, T. D. (1994, March 25). Student racism prompts reaction: North hills district to frame racial policy after recent incidents. Pittsburgh Post-Gazette.

11   Williams, T. D. (1994, April 6). North hills offers plan to combat school bias. Pittsburgh Post-Gazette.

12   Ibid.

13   Trent, M., Dooley,, D. G., & Dougé, J. (2019, August 1). The impact of racism on child and adolescent health. Re-

trieved March 29, 2020, from https://pediatrics.aappublications.org/content/144/2/e20191765.

14   Ross, D. (1978). Track 23.

15   Joan Ryan

16   Amelia E. Barr

17   Ross, D. (1978). Track 23.

18   WebMD LLC. (2018). Is It PTSD, depression, or both? Retrieved from https://www.webmd.com/depression/depression-ptsd-vs-depression#1

19   U.S. News and World Report

20   Ross, D. (1978). Track 23.

21   Coleman, M. A. (2016). Bi-polar faith: A Black woman's journey with depression and faith. Minneapolis, MN: Fortress Press.

22   Ibid.

23   Meet Pastor Elijah Sebuchu. (n.d.). Retrieved March 29, 2020, from https://handsofloveusa.org/who-we-are/meet-pastor-elijah/.

24   Withers, B. (1971). Track 3.

25   Solchany, J. E. (2001). Promoting Maternal Mental Health During Pregnancy: Theory, Practice & Intervention. Seattle, WA: NCAST-AVENUW.

26   Ibid.

27   The breakfast club. (1985). Retrieved March 29, 2020, from https://www.imdb.com/title/tt0088847/.

28   Emory university hospital at wesley woods. (n.d.). Retrieved March 29, 2020, from https://www.emoryhealthcare.org/locations/hospitals/emory-university-hospital-wesley-woods/index.html.

29   Douglas, S. (2017, September 15). Neuropsychological evaluations 101. Retrieved March 29, 2020, from https://www.psychologytoday.com/us/blog/promoting-academic-success/201709/neuropsychological-evaluations-101

30   Daniel Goleman

31   Harris Parris, A. (2017). Self care matters: a revolutionary's approach (K. Brundidge, Ed.). United States of America: YBF Publishing, LLC.

32   National Sleep Foundation. (n.d.). Sleep deprivation and postpartum depression: How to tell the difference. Retrieved March 29, 2020, from https://www.sleepfoundation.org/articles/sleep-deprivation-and-postpartum-depression-how-tell-difference

33   MyHealthfinder. (n.d.). Get enough sleep. Retrieved March 29, 2020, from https://healthfinder.gov/healthtopics/category/everyday-healthy-living/mental-health-and-relationship/get-enough-sleep

34   Dennett, C. (2020, January 18). Why is it healthy to eat three meals a day? Retrieved March 29, 2020, from https://www.livestrong.com/article/43876-eat-three-meals-day

35   Pfizer. (2020). The importance of taking your medications correctly. Retrieved March 29, 2020, from https://www.pfizer.com/health/senior_health/taking_medicines

36   Bowers, E. S. (n.d.). 10 signs your antidepressant isn't working [Everyday Health]. Retrieved March 29, 2020, from https://www.everydayhealth.com/depression/signs-your-antidepressant-isnt-working.aspx

37   Kleiman, K. (2019). Good Moms Have Scary Thoughts: A Healing Guide to the Secret Fears of New Mothers. Sanger, CA: Familius.

38   The Institute for Integrative Nutrition Self Care Journal

39   Harris Parris, A. (2017). Self care matters: a revolution-